THE LORD'S PRAYER

THE LORD'S PRAYER

an exposition

by

WALTER LÜTHI

Translated by

KURT SCHOENENBERGER

JOHN KNOX PRESS

RICHMOND, VIRGINIA

Published in Great Britain by Oliver and Boyd Ltd.,
Edinburgh and London, and in the United States
of America by John Knox Press, Richmond, Virginia.

Library of Congress Catalog Card Number: 62-7170

A translation of *Das Unservater*: *Eine Auslegung*
by Walter Lüthi, first published in 1946 by
Verlag Friedrich Reinhardt AG. Basle.

The Scripture quotations in this book are from
the Revised Standard Version of the Bible,
copyright 1946 and 1952 by the Division of
Christian Education, National Council of the
Churches of Christ in the U.S.A., and used
by permission.

ENGLISH EDITION
Second Printing 1962

Contents

Our Father who art in heaven,
Hallowed be thy name.
Thy kingdom come,
Thy will be done,
   On earth as it is in heaven.
Give us this day our daily bread;
And forgive us our debts,
   As we also have forgiven our debtors;
And lead us not into temptation,
But deliver us from evil.
For thine is the kingdom
And the power
And the glory, forever.
Amen.

                        (Mt. VI.9–13)

The Father

Our Father who art in heaven . . .

WHEN the tremendous bloodshed of the last war was followed by the dropping of that new bomb on a far eastern island empire, not only inanimate things were shaken for a moment, but also many human hearts. And perhaps this shock had to come so that we should not be lulled once more into a deceptive confidence in peace. For we had just begun to look round for building sites for a better world; we had just begun to feel more or less at ease again; and we were getting used to the idea that we had survived the earthquake once more. And now, instead of this, we have to accustom ourselves to the increased probability of inconceivably more powerful convulsions in the more distant future. Indeed this new means of destruction which, it is to be feared, will soon be superseded,[1] seems to us to have revealed something of the true nature of this world. Perhaps the earth is not as suitable for a building site and foundation as we thought we could take for granted a short while ago. So if we are looking round for firmer land for building, then we would be well advised to leave this earth quite out of consideration. For this latest earthquake might mean once and for all the end of everything that until recently we have dared to call security. But the Lord provides for this end of all security on earth when He teaches His own to pray to a God who is in *Heaven*.

Furthermore it is part of the nature of this earth that it will become "dust and ashes". The works of men are subject to a law of dust, so to speak. Still, up till now it has

[1] These sermons were first delivered in 1946.

I

usually been years, decades, or even centuries before the shroud of decay settled over the works of man and finally reduced them to dust; but human memory is lost in the centuries. So is it surprising that men constantly forget the condition of the world? Lately, however, the dust character of the earth has been proved scientifically and demonstrated to mankind as if in a laboratory experiment. No centuries are necessary now, nor even a year: at the pressure of a finger on a little button a human city becomes a pillar of dust. Have we any comment to make on this latest achievement in the technique of destruction? What more can we say than that there is a Heaven above the earth, a Heaven above all the dust: "Our Father, who art in heaven".

And not only this earth, but also its inhabitant, man, is dust and ashes: "Earth to earth, dust to dust"—surely we have always known what we are; but what we did not know until now is that we not only are dust and become dust, but that we are capable of creating dust. We have become capable of creating and raising up swirling clouds of dust, so far to a height of 40,000 feet above the earth. What master producers of dust we are, what world champions of annihilation! What an abyss of nothingness opens up before us! But above atoms, and above the splitting of the atom, and above nothingness, there is Heaven. And Heaven is above man too, above the champion of destruction. Here we are beginning to have an insight into what it means to pray, for here we are reduced to the groan of distress and the cry born of deep need; but also to the last hope, the *spes ultima*, in which we say once more: "Our Father, who art in heaven".

Although strange and paradoxical, it is significant that in this hellish war a generation that had lost sight of Heaven was compelled for the first time for many years to see the struggle for the balance of power transferred to the skies. Perhaps it is also not quite by chance that this generation, drunk with worldliness, has had to hear so much about "air superiority", and that novels of the war in the air are so widely read today.

At any rate no other generation within living memory has looked up to the heavens by day and night as often as we have. Strange though it may seem, it is a long time since this generation was afraid of what comes from above, and we had long ago forgotten what it was like to long for help from above. Does it not give us food for thought that of all people this heavenless generation, who had only a superior, pitying smile left for the blessing that comes from above, came to fear or expect death or life from above, whether they wanted to or not? But in view of the rediscovery of the heavens beyond us, we cannot suppress the quiet wish: if only this generation would reach the stage of rediscovering the real and true Heaven, not the sky of the night fighter and the death-laden bomber, but the Heaven of the angels, the Heaven of God, the Heaven of the Ascension, that Heaven that Christ means when He teaches His own to pray: "Our Father, who art in *heaven*".

However horrified we are at ourselves, however much we begin to avert our eyes from the earth and to look beyond the earth, we must guard against contemptuously despising this poor earth. Before God we have no right to self-contempt. It is understandable and pardonable if, in the face of discoveries of this kind, we turn away from the earth in horror and disgust and begin to seek refuge in the heavens. Only we must not make the mistake of thinking that God does the same thing. If the Holy Scriptures tell us anything, then it is this: that God loves the earth, He loves it in spite of the fact that it is dust and ashes; indeed, He loves it for that very reason. It is just because the earth is in such a critical state that God turns His eyes towards it instead of looking away from it. And instead of fleeing this earth that we should like to renounce, God does the opposite and seeks it. Like a mother with her problem child,

God turns His whole attention, His wisdom, His love, and His heart to the earth. God does not deny His work. Any other craftsman would be ashamed and would abandon his creation if it behaved like this: but God does not deny His work, because He loves it. It is not because of its lovable condition, but because He takes pity on its hateful condition that God acknowledges the earth as His. God loves the earth even if, and just because, it trembles; God loves the sun even if it burns things up; God loves the stream even if it overflows its banks; He loves the lightning even if it sets things on fire; the lion even if it plunders; the dog even if it barks and bites; God loves the mountains and the hills; He loves the houses, villages, and towns of men even if they fall down and bury their occupants beneath them; God loves the earth, for it is His earth and He is its Father. But how can we explain this? This is something that is beyond explanation. To try to explain would not make things any clearer, but would only make them more incomprehensible. All that can be done is to state a fact. There is a love that can do what no other love can do, and that is the love of Him who is not only the Lord above the dust, but also the Lord in the dust. It is the love of Him whom Christ teaches us to call our *Father*.

But there is good reason for God's recognition of His creatures and for His refusal to deny His Fatherhood even of the children who have turned out badly. It does not follow as a matter of course that it is God we are addressing as Father when we say the Lord's Prayer. A great man once said that when he said the Lord's Prayer he first of all thought of another father, namely his earthly one: "When I say it, I first of all think of my late father, how good he was and how he loved to give me things" (Matthias Claudius). This association with the physical father bespeaks the piety of a great mind, but in this connexion it must be applied with caution. For if our earthly fathers were evidence that the Holy God in Heaven is our Father, then the millions of children who cannot refer to an earthly father because they have never known one would have to be pitied. Or then we would think of children like those who lived next door to us when I was a child, whose father was addicted to drink. However engrossed we were in our play, there was one thing that they never overlooked: the approach of evening. The nearer the sun dipped towards the horizon, the more frequently did this or that playmate from next door hesitate and glance furtively towards the lane along which their father would come home after work. And then, when the warning cry rang out; "Father's coming! Father's coming!" the happy group would scatter, each child hiding from his father like chickens when the cock approaches, none of them wanting to be the first to be seen, addressed, or perhaps seized by their father. Innumerable children live like that today, children for whom the thought of their earthly father related to belief in the Father in Heaven would be a hindrance rather than a help. Nevertheless Matthias Claudius was right in not daring to approach the Lord's Prayer directly, but instead seeking mediation. In order to say the Lord's Prayer we definitely need mediation. For, truth to tell, without it we human beings would all have to fear our Father in Heaven and take cover from Him, as once the first man hid from God after his fall. The call, "Father is coming!" would be a cry of terror for all of us, not because God the Father is bad, brutal, and unjust, like so many human fathers, but because we, His children, are bad. Because of our sins we would all have good reason to scatter like chickens before the hawk at the coming of God the Father. But no physical father, however good he may be, can provide this mediation for us in our approach to God: that needs another mediator. If today, instead of running off in terror, we can approach God in whole-hearted childlike trust in spite of the fact that we are wicked children, then the explanation is that Christ has intervened. Christ was not ashamed to become

our Brother, the Brother of atom-splitters. In Christ God
who is Lord above the dust has become Lord in the dust.
The man who wants to say the Lord's Prayer, and who
prays in earnest, cannot do so without the Son. This
prayer is seriously conceivable only if it is taken as a gift
from the hand of the Son. Therefore when you say the
Lord's Prayer, think diligently of how Christmas came
about, and how the Father in Heaven gave up His Dearest;
think of how Good Friday came about, and how the
heavenly Father lets you look right into His compassionate
heart. And when you say the Lord's Prayer, think of all
the miracles of that love that happened when Jesus Christ
was on earth; think of Easter and the Ascension, Pentecost
and His return with all the holy promises for this poor
earth and to us men that have still to be fulfilled. When
you say the Lord's Prayer it is foolish, indeed dangerous
and sinful, to think first of all in gratitude of anyone else
at all except that Man on the Cross, to whom each one of
us, "our late fathers" included, owes everything. Through
the Son and through Him alone God in Heaven became
our *Father*.

Through Christ God taught us to call Him the eternal
Father, and through Christ we were given the blessed name
of children. And for this very reason that we are allowed
to call God our Father and ourselves His children, we are
brothers. All those who are allowed to believe in Christ
through the influence of the Holy Spirit are brothers and
sisters; that is what believers are. Year after year, when
the new classes enrol for instruction, we are faced with
those pathetic only children who bear in their hearts the
unsatisfied longing for brothers and sisters. The man who
awakens to faith in Christ through the Holy Spirit is confronted with the miracle that he is no longer an "only child"
and now has brothers and sisters. All over the world, in
America, in Russia, in the remotest parts of Turkey and
Japan, and in Germany too, there lives a host of brothers

in faith whose numbers are known to God alone, and who say the Lord's Prayer with you. They say it in different languages, it is true: but they all pray through the one Christ to the one God in the one Holy Spirit. But the love of God does not want to stop half way, which it would be doing if it were to confine itself to the circle of believers; no, God wants to extend His Father-love to the very ends of the earth. The love of God does not let itself be limited to the community of the believing. Just as the Father lets all believers experience His love through the Son, so He wants to testify His love to all men through those who believe; yes, He wants to draw the whole of Creation into His fatherly mercy. It is because God also wants to be the Father of those who do not believe in Him that believers cannot exclude other people when they say the Lord's Prayer: on the contrary, they include everything that bears a human face and their prayer embraces the whole of Creation. Thus the Lord's Prayer is the true and noblest prayer of intercession. Although the community prays within its own circle, it embraces all men and all Creation when it says, "*Our* Father".

But the fact that God's Father-love comes to us through the mediation of the Son is a source of vexation to us. We should prefer Father-love that is not tied to Christ; we should like "love for nothing", and want to be unconditional, free brothers without becoming children of God; we should like a brotherhood of men that ignores and excludes brotherhood of faith. In place of the brotherhood that we are given as a gift we prefer a man-made fraternity. What was the wave of nationalism that has only just passed if not a human attempt of this kind in the name of the nation to form a human brotherhood which excluded all those who were "of no use to the nation"! Thus there arose a narrow, deformed, and brutal brotherhood of men which spread death and destruction. And it will not be long before a new wave will be under way, a brotherhood of all nations, a brotherhood in the name of the International. It will be a brotherhood of international agreements, of international matches, international motorways and huge airports, and, it is to be feared, once more a brotherhood that excludes Christ and therefore once again doomed from the start. But the Lord's Prayer is more than just national and more than international: it is Christ's gift of Grace to the community that prays, on behalf of all people and the whole of Creation, "*Our* Father, who art in heaven".

"Heaven", "Father", and "our", these are words whose meaning we men shall have to learn anew after this earthquake. But it will be no easy thing for us. Difficulties will hinder our acceptance of this gift. We cannot now simply begin to say the Lord's Prayer as if we had always done so, and as if things had always run smoothly between us and the Father. Some time ago I heard of a father who had been separated from his family by the war for many years, and when he first met his children again they did not recognise him any more. Everyone was painfully embarrassed, and the mother had to tell the children to shake hands with the man standing there in front of them, for after all he was their father. The same kind of embarrassment affects people today when they are told that God in Heaven is their Father, for they do not know Him any more. The Father whom they should welcome is a stranger to them. But the Father in Heaven has not been away at the war: we men were at war, long before this wretched earthquake began. The Father in Heaven was not away from us; He has always been with us: no, we were away from Him, because we are children who have run away from home. We loved foreign lands more than our Father's house, and so became a generation estranged from the Father. Consequently there is a terrifyingly large number of sons of men who can no longer say, "Our Father, who art in heaven". To all of them the appeal goes out: Come, turn back! Come home from abroad! Come home to the Father, for there is peace now; not peace for any one generation: in Christ there is eternal peace. Come, children, give this Man your hands and welcome Him, for it has been a dreadful misunderstanding that you were supposed to have no Father and to be nobody's children; because we know Christ, that is simply not true any more and will never, never be true again. Come and throw yourselves into your Father's arms and say, "Father, I have sinned, and am no longer worthy to be called your son; treat me as one of your hired servants". For Christ's sake you can now pray heartily and fervently, "Our Father, who art in heaven . . ."

B

The Name

GOD has a name. The misery on this earth is nameless, the evil among men is nameless, for the powers of darkness love to be without a name. Nameless, anonymous letters, letters without signatures are usually vulgar. But God is no writer of anonymous letters; God puts His name to everything that He does, effects, and says; God has no need to fear the light of day. The Devil loves anonymity, but God has a name. He did not get this name by chance; in fact He did not receive it at all: He gave it to Himself because He wants to have a name. For him, name does not mean noise and smoke that cloud the splendour of Heaven; His name is His sign, the sign that shows that He is the true God; His name is His signature, so to speak, His monogram, His seal, His stamp (His trademark, if you will!)—whatever bears this stamp is God's. God would certainly have had the power to be nameless; but because He loves clarity and hates obscurity He preferred not to be a nameless God.

And His name is holy; in other words it does not need to be made holy or hallowed: it is holy already. It is not as if God were in need of something that He does not possess already, something that He has to wait for us to provide for Him. His name always was holy; it is holy and will be in eternity. His name is holy; that means that this name belongs to Him and to no other. God is the only bearer of this name; He has the monopoly of it, in a manner of speaking; it is in the literal sense of the word His proper name. Therefore this first petition of the Lord's Prayer corresponds to the first of the Ten Commandments, which is also concerned with the fact that God is unique and that there is no other besides or before Him. His name alone is holy. In Heaven that has always been known, and that is why no prayer for the hallowing of God's name is ever heard there; this is a prayer for the earth and for us men. We hear something else from Heaven; there there is worship and rejoicing: "Holy, holy, holy is the Lord of hosts; the whole earth is full of his glory" (Is. vi.3).

And now God has decided to take a step that is difficult to understand. He makes His name known not only, as we might expect, to the angels and the saints in Heaven, but generally, to the whole earth, and He has given us permission to use it. God has put His name into circulation, so to speak, among us men here on earth, and has thus put it at our mercy. Even humanly speaking it is a risk to give away your signature, because you never know what might become of it; if the signature gets into the wrong hands you have no more control over it, and it can be misused or even forged at any time. Has the same thing happened to God with His name? Had He no foreboding of what would happen in the days when He put His holy signature into circulation in this unholy earth? Was He unsuspecting and ignorant of the danger and misuse to which He was exposing His good name? Why should He not have known that? If He did it in spite of this, He did so out of love. He loves us so much that He put aside all anxiety about the holiness of His name; so much that He even put mercy before His holiness. He was so deeply touched by our wretchedness here below that instead of confining His name to the angels and saints up there above the stars He relinquished it to us men, knowing into what dirty ears, on to what unclean lips, into what stained hearts and into what bad company His name would fall. It is with good reason that, as we have seen, He is called "Our Father"! The very fact that He gave His name to us shows how much and how completely He is our Father. But now, even if He has put aside His holiness out of pity, we must take care not to think that the holiness of His name has therefore become cheap and a matter of indifference to Him. On the contrary, even if it has pleased Him to put His mercy before His holiness, then that is His concern and not ours; as far as we are concerned, the warning still holds good: "You shall not take the name of the Lord your God in vain; for the Lord will not hold him guiltless who takes His name in vain" (Ex. xx.7). In other words, anyone who misuses the name of God the Father is misusing His kindness.

What God's holy name has to endure here on earth in spite of His warning defies description. The history of His name on earth is one of downright suffering. You sometimes come across a coin that has become worn away and unrecognisable as a result of passing through many hands. Now coins can be taken out of circulation at will: but what a worn coin the name of God has become among us religious people! That is why this first petition applies primarily to the Church: may His name no longer be a worn coin but may its outline, edges, and stamping be clearly defined again! When you touch one of those torn, greasy, and sticky ten-shilling notes, how badly you feel you want to wash your hands! Yet it is only decaying paper. But how torn, greasy, and sticky the talk about God has become among us religious people! And yet His name is hóly, holy, holy. It sometimes happens that money is devalued, and there is inflation. There is also a kind of inflation in the Church, an inflation of the Word, so that it has no value any more and becomes empty. Indeed, just as a gang of criminals may begin to circulate false money, so there is also a kind of forgery in the Church among us pious people, both in and out of the pulpit. In this case, however, God knows it is not gangs of criminals who carry on this spiritual forgery—which of us has never taken part in it? Which of us is not one of those "people of unclean lips" (Is. vi.5) who circulate false coin even in the words of prayer? Who is not judged by the words: "for the Lord will not hold him guiltless who takes his name in vain"? Let us guard against comforting ourselves too easily with the thought that after all God's primary desire is to be merciful and that He is called Father, for what is His free Grace is never our right. If God for His part puts the name of Father first, then we for our part must put the name of Lord first and respect it. There is no getting away from it, God will not hold him guiltless who misuses His name.

And so this first petition of the Lord's Prayer has led us to realise our own poverty and helplessness. Now we are capable of understanding how very much this first plea coincides not only with the first Commandment but also with the first of the Beatitudes, about the poor in spirit, those very people who have nothing left to boast about before God. When we are confronted with the name of God, the likes of us can only be poor. We are beginning to comprehend why these words about the name of God are not only a command but at the same time a prayer. Before the holy name of God we are in a situation where we can only be afraid and call for help. Let us call for help then! "Help, Lord; we constantly desecrate Thy name and bring shame after shame upon Thee. Help, Lord, so that Thy name may be hallowed. Admittedly I do not know who can hallow it, but grant that it may be hallowed. I myself cannot hallow it and, as far as I can see, nor can any of my neighbours; but help, Lord, so that Thy name may be hallowed nevertheless!" So it can happen, and definitely does happen with the help of the Holy Spirit, that this prayer gives the believer no peace, but begins to accompany him like a sigh, day after day, until all other prayers fade before this one: "Lord, only let Thy name be hallowed!" With the help of the Holy Spirit it becomes a strangely selfless request, and all personal interests and urgent everyday matters recede and make way for it. It was certainly not by chance that Christ gave this particular petition the first place in His prayer, and the Holy Spirit can make it move into first place in your life too. And you may even become filled with zeal for God's name. We all know the zealous upholders of God's holiness in the Old and New Testaments. We all know of the men in the history of the Church in whom the zealous love of the holiness of God was revealed. We all know of Calvin, who gave this first petition of the Lord's Prayer first place, its rightful place, as long as he lived. All of them were so eager to see the name of God hallowed that they gave glory to God alone: *"Soli deo gloria"*!

At this stage the question becomes even more pressing: who in the Church can endure the holy name of God? Is it not a consuming fire that kills everyone who ventures near it? The plea for God's holiness would undoubtedly kill us, just as Ananias and Saphira were killed for their spiritual forgery, if it were not for one thing: God Himself answered this prayer by sending the One who is the great exception. The name of God entered through His ear into His holy heart and crossed His pure lips: dirtied and debased as it was when He found it on earth, He took it unto Himself. He withdrew all the worn and forged coins, melted them down and minted them anew. There on the Cross He bore all the misuse of the name of God, and also suffered all the punishment for it. On the Cross and there alone God's name is hallowed. We said that the history of this name on earth is one of downright suffering, and sure enough it has led to a Passion in the true sense of the word. The name of God came back from the Cross purified and shining as on the first day, and was once more put into circulation among men. We are offered an insight into the extent to which the Lord, in the time of His Passion, is moved and engrossed by the name of God when we read Christ's High-Priestly prayer in the fourth Gospel where, faced with the prospect of the Cross, He prays, "I made known to them thy name", and "For their sake I consecrate myself, that they also may be consecrated in truth" (Jn. XVII.19, 26). He took upon Himself the misused name of God; but for this act of obedience God gave Him a "name which is above every name" (Phil. II.9).

And we, God's children and heirs, are also offered a share in this name that is hallowed by Christ, for He Himself says, "I consecrate myself, that they *also* may be consecrated". We are all endowed with this name through the gift of Baptism. We are baptised in the name of the Father, the Son, and the Holy Spirit. It is the holy name and not the misused one that we are endowed with at Baptism: we are taken into, we might even say enveloped in, the holiness of His name. In this way Christ lets us take a share in His fulfilment of this petition. Therefore we in the Church can pray without despairing, and in confidence and trust, for the hallowing of His name, because we are protected by Baptism: His hallowed name has been bestowed upon us from the Cross as a gift of His kingly majesty.

Yes, we can bear this name; we can take it home with us and can go on bearing it for the rest of our days. But I hope that we do not bear it in such a way as to give rise to the sort of complaint that I heard from an atheist the other day, who said bitterly that good church-goers are bad neighbours. It is only too often true that good church-goers are bad neighbours; but how very different things would be if we were accompanied at every step and at every turn by the knowledge that we are baptised in God's hallowed name. Surely if we take Baptism seriously it means that the holiness of the divine name will never forsake us, and that we are bound to give glory to God alone. It means that we have and bring up children to the glory of God; we can wash napkins, learn Latin, or break stones to the glory of God. It means that morning after morning we can go to work protected by God's hallowed

name. What a glorious new meaning work acquires now!
We should have to recognise the name of God, His holiness,
and His love in every day-labourer. Our first consideration
on starting a job would no longer be success and gain, but
the hallowing of God's name. What a heavenly light would
shine on our factories and our offices, our council chambers
and our homes up and down the land!

Finally, this first petition of the Lord's Prayer has a
special relevance for the generation of today. A few years
ago there died a Christian woman who had been tied to her
bed for many years by a severe illness. In her hours of
solitude she prayed a great deal for other people, both for
the community and for individuals. Her prayers of
intercession were interesting for their decided form, which
however was more than mere pattern, for whenever she
had brought all her requests for a particular person before
the throne of God, she would close her prayer with the
words: "and may he become silent before Thee". And
then she would pray for someone else, and again close with
the remarkable, almost formal words, "and may he become
silent before Thee". Becoming silent before God was
evidently of the greatest importance to her: this sorely
afflicted woman regarded it as essential to the hallowing of
God's name. This kind of hallowing has special application
for us today. The misery that has passed over the earth
has left a great bitterness behind in the minds of innumerable
people: a bitterness that grows like a snowball, not only
against men but above all against God. Why has God
done this? Does God let such things happen? Where is
your God then? If you are God, then come down and
help. God is dead. That is the sort of querulous outburst
that people give vent to in their bitterness, and their indignation is like a clenched fist raised to the sky. This
rebellion culminates in a wave of suicide passing through
our ranks. After all, suicide is so often a final gesture of
defiance against Heaven, the defiance of despair, the last

trick that a man thinks he must play on Heaven, by throwing his life at the feet of the Creator like a parcel, rejected with bitter scorn, the life that He hallowed and for which He died. The man who has rebelled in this way and in the end falls silent before God like Job, and repents, "God, thy way is holy", is hallowing God's name in a special way. When his accusations turn to self-accusation; when in the end even the bitter self-accusation is silenced before the Cross; when he concedes that God alone is and always has been right, then the rebel becomes silent before God, and through his silence hallows God's name. In a bunker near Cologne, in which some hunted men had hidden for a time, the following inscription was found on the wall: 'I believe in the sun even if it is not shining; I believe in God even if He is silent; I believe in love even if it is hidden". That is how a sorely afflicted man hallowed the name of his God. The Christian, however, can hallow God's name by confessing: I believe in the light, for Christ is the light in the darkness; I believe in God, for He spoke in Christ and is not silent; I believe in love, for love appeared on the Cross.

The Kingdom

Thy Kingdom come . . .

AT first it seems quite astonishing that we should pray
for the coming of God's Kingdom. Can it be that
there is even one tiny spot on earth, let alone in
Heaven, where God is not already present, and which He
has yet to reach? How can this second petition of the
Lord's Prayer be reconciled with the omnipresence of
God as we read of it in the Psalm: "If I ascend to heaven,
thou art there! If I make my bed in Sheol, thou art there!
If I take the wings of the morning and dwell in the utter-
most parts of the sea, even there thy hand shall lead me, and
thy right hand shall hold me"? (Ps. cxxxix.8-10).

God's omnispresence is not to be understood in the
sense that He has to be everywhere, as if He were bound
to be in every stone, in every blade of grass, and in every
drop of rain; as if He were, so to speak, the prisoner of
His own omnipresence. No, God is the Lord: He is not
compelled to behave in any particular way. God has kept
His freedom of movement; God can come near and go
away; God can give Himself and take Himself away; and
if God wants to come and go, who will prevent Him?
The correct interpretation of God's omnipresence is that
there is no place in Heaven or on earth or in Hell that could
keep God back if He wanted to go, or prevent His coming
if He wanted to come. All doors are open to His staying
or coming or going. Therefore there is already good reason
for saying this prayer, which does admittedly sound
astonishing at first: "Thy kingdom come", do not forsake
us, stay with us; and if you have gone away, then come
back, "Thy kingdom come".

And the most terrible thing of all has actually happened: God has gone: as we hear so often in the Psalms and the Prophets, God has turned His back; He has turned away His countenance from this tiny province of His Kingdom, away from this earth. No doubt God had His reasons for going. He knows why, and we should really know too, because we are to blame that God has estranged Himself for a time from this province, and has withdrawn from it. It is our fault that this earth today is not the paradise that a province in the Kingdom of God should be, but a battle-ground of men and powers, an arena of war on land, on the sea, and in the air, and soon probably in the stratosphere too. We are to blame that God has forsaken us.

But God left us one thing, and that is the memory that even this God-forsaken province belongs to the Kingdom of God. Through His servants He has reminded us again and again that we belong to it. He has held out to the inhabitants of this God-forsaken province the prospect that He might return some day and that He will one day re-enter this planet. When in His wisdom He deemed it good; when in His freedom He decided to be merciful; "when the time was fulfilled" He sent His Son. And the very first words that Christ spoke when He began to preach were, "The kingdom of heaven is at hand" (Mt. IV.17). In the course of His ministry, however, He went so far as to add, "The kingdom of God has come upon you" (Mt. XII.28).

Thus in Jesus Christ this once-lost province is incorporated again into the Kingdom of God. In Jesus Christ the Kingdom of God is here, irrevocably here. Admittedly He goes to the Cross, but He does so in order to bear and take away everything that has happened between men and God since time immemorial. Admittedly He cries, "My God, my God, why hast thou forsaken me?" (Mt. XXVII.46), but surely only in order to take upon Himself all the God-forsakenness of this earth, and so that it may never, never be God-forsaken again. In Jesus Christ the Kingdom has come. In Jesus Christ every blade of grass, every drop of rain, and every sparrow on the rooftops is God's. In Jesus Christ "the earth is the Lord's" and all that is in it. In Jesus Christ we are the Lord's people. All power is given to Him, not only in heaven but also on earth: the angels in Heaven have to bow before Him; death on earth has to give way to Him; devils tremble before Him: in Jesus Christ the whole of this old world is judged and saved.

That gives us a second reason to be astonished that we need to say this prayer at all, and that it is Christ of all people who puts it on our lips. Does this mean that His Kingdom is not complete after all? Is it only partly here? Have we rejoiced too soon again, as so often before? It is complete, for Christ's going to the Cross was complete. As surely as Christ took all the God-forsakenness upon Himself, His Kingdom has come. As surely as Christ took all the God-forsakenness upon Himself, His Kingdom has come. As surely as He went to the grave; as surely as He descended into Hell; as surely as He rose again, God's Kingdom is here among us now. The whole thing would be a lie; all the Prophets and the Apostles would have lied if the Kingdom of God had not come to earth in Jesus Christ. And if all the same we still have to pray, "Thy kingdom come", then once again there is good reason for it, namely that Christ forces no man to accept His Kingdom; under all circumstances He respects the desire of the Christian to be free. For we men do not belong to the Kingdom of God like a raindrop, or a stone, or a sparrow on the roof; man does not belong to the Kingdom by nature or by fate: the Cross and the Resurrection and the Kingdom of Christ on earth put us men, as distinct from things, into a position where we have to make a choice and a decision. Do we want to believe in God or not? It is through faith that we enter the Kingdom of God. As human beings we are not attached to God's Kingdom like the apple to the

branch by means of a stalk: we can only be united with
the Kingdom of God by faith. Therefore faith is the decisive
factor here, hence the question: "Do you believe or do you
not? Do you want to belong to the Kingdom of God
through faith or do you not?" So the fundamental question
posed by this second petition of the Lord's Prayer is the
question of faith.

But here we have a third reason to be astonished, or
even horrified: we cannot belong to the Kingdom of God
in this world, even though it is here. It is here but we do
not belong to it—what a dreadful thought! And we
cannot believe either, because there are any number of
ways out of it. The man who does not believe does not
belong to the Kingdom of God in spite of the fact that it is
here. But what else is there if we do not belong to it? If
a man does not believe and therefore does not want to
belong to the Kingdom of Christ, he comes under the
dominion of the power that death and the Devil are still
allowed to have in this world. He is then exposed to those
forces, principalities, and demons, which are hostile to the
Kingdom. You see, either we are subjects of Jesus Christ
in faith, or then in unbelief subjects of the money bag,
subjects of the military idol, subjects of the desires in our
own blood, subjects of every topical idea and fearful error,
subjects of those half-forces which still have a bit of power
left.

All the same it is a vexation to us that they still possess
this bit of power, which is considerable by human reckoning. We can understand the child who, for the first time
in his young life, saw a man lying dead drunk in the street,
and who was so deeply upset that he would neither rest nor
go to sleep, but kept on asking, "Father, why was that man
like that?" "Because he had been drinking alcohol."
"What is alcohol, father?" "Alcohol is poison." "But
why is there poison?" Here the father was in a cleft stick
and had to admit, "Because there is a Devil, my child".

"But why has the Devil not died, father?" That is the direct reasoning of a child's mind; if only we could be like children! Who cannot understand this child's fearful question why the Devil has not died? Why has death still so much power left? Ultimately there is only one answer: Death and the Devil are certainly given enough power to be stronger than us men, but not enough power to be stronger than Christ. Christ is the stronger. It is not true that there are two equal kingdoms in this world, Christ's Kingdom and Satan's kingdom. Even though time and again it may seem that the kingdom of the Devil is superior to Christ's, it is not even equal to it. It is not true that the course of the world is an undecided tug-of-war between Christ and the Devil, and that we men are pulled to and fro between them. The tug-of-war has been decided, decided in Christ's favour, and therefore in ours. It is not a case of combatants face to face: here the defeated opponent faces his Conqueror, who is and always will be Christ. That is the sense in which we pray, "Thy kingdom come", and the sense in which we sing, "Thy Kingdom come, O God, Thy rule, O Christ, begin". A missionary who has now spent six years behind the wire of a prison camp understood this very well when he wrote recently, "Every day we make clear to the Devil something that he does not like hearing, namely that he has been defeated".

But what is the situation as regards faith? We have seen that it is faith alone that gives us a share in the Kingdom, so would we not all like to believe, and thus belong to it? But what about the decision to believe? Can we simply do it to order? Do we know nothing of the power of our habits of resistance? Nevertheless we dare to say, "Believe now; decide now", for everything depends on our believing. We have every sympathy with the man who cried out in his distress, "I believe, help my unbelief!" (Mk. ix.24).

That reminds us that all the time we have been talking about prayer. "Thy kingdom come" is a prayer. Our prayer for the coming of His Kingdom is to be understood in the very first place as a request for faith: "May faith come". It has often been said that we are concerned with faith in all the other petitions of the Lord's Prayer, but that what the second one is concerned with is works. No. Here we are also concerned only with faith. This petition too is first and foremost a petition for faith. May faith come; may faith come to us who are always weak in faith. Holy Spirit, waken faith in my child, waken faith in my neighbour who does not believe at all yet. And strengthen the faith of all who believe, so that it does not die. For the distress and misery of our time does not originate from the fact that the Kingdom of God is not here, but from the fact that we do not believe in it, or that our faith is inadequate. That is why the first aspect of this second petition of the Lord's Prayer is a plea for faith. Give us faith! Take away our unbelief! Is there any prayer that could be more urgent, more comprehensive, and therefore more effective than the prayer for faith?

But faith comes from hearing the Word. And so this prayer, "Thy kingdom come", includes another, "Thy Word come". But is it not already here? Is the Word not current in the Church? Many things are current, but it is questionable whether they are always the Word of God. Thy Word come! Let us no longer hear our own words, but let Thy Word come down upon us. Let Thy Word come upon us in such a way that it overwhelms us. Let Thy Word come; the Word that is like a consuming fire and like a hammer that breaks the rock in pieces. May Thy Word come like the morning and the evening rain. May Thy Word come. Take away our empty talk and give us the authority of Thy Word. Is there any conceivable prayer that could be more comprehensive and therefore more urgent than this one?

And with the Word go the Sacraments, especially Baptism. Baptism too is practised in the Church, and yet

it is so far from us: in the experience of most of us Baptism
is remote, certainly as regards time. What a contrast with
the central position that Baptism took at that first Pentecost,
when the people asked, "What shall we do?" and Peter, in
that highly significant hour, answered quite simply, "Repent, and be baptised every one of you in the name of
Jesus Christ for the forgiveness of your sins; and you shall
receive the gift of the Holy Spirit" (Acts II.38). That is
true Baptism. That is what it should be! May it come;
may Baptism come to us and our children, Baptism by the
Holy Spirit, Baptism of the Spirit and of fire.

And the Holy Communion is another Sacrament from
which the community has become estranged today. It is
often only a dozen steps to the Table and yet how many
can no longer take those few steps! The barriers to the
altar are supposed to have been done away with; but other
barriers have come: walls, ditches, and obstacles which
bar the community's way to the Communion. The distance
between us and the Lord's Table has become so great. But
if we can no longer reach it, let us at least pray, "Thy
Communion come"; may it come to us; let it come to
pass that the community can no longer bear to stay away
from the Table. May Thy Communion come, so that
it may again become the centre, the centre of life, the
centre of the family, the centre of the community, the
centre of the people and of the nations that are so dreadfully
without a central core. May Thy Sacrament come upon
us and to us: that is what we mean when we pray, "Thy
kingdom come".

Is this really what we pray? Is not our basic weakness
revealed in our praying as nowhere else? Do we pray,
"Thy kingdom come", or do not ninety per cent of our
prayers run, "*My* kingdom come"? Is our own self not
at the centre of all our prayers? Should not the Kingdom
be the focal point? Do not our prayers in particular suffer
from a strange spiritual inbreeding, since they all revolve

round our own selves? How very different our prayers will be when they come to us and upon us from God and once again have the Kingdom as their centre. Yes, even prayer itself has to come upon us again, because we are in the position where the disciples once found themselves when they approached Christ with the request: "Lord, teach us to pray" (Lk. xi.i). We must learn to pray the Lord's Prayer again; our prayers must grow healthy again in the Lord's Prayer, with the Kingdom as its centre.

So in a nutshell, "Thy kingdom come" comprises: may prayer come, may Communion, Baptism, and the Word come, so that faith may come.

It is possible that some people may be disappointed by this and ask, "Is that all"? But if they are disappointed they did not hear what we said, for we did not mean that the whole world should become a pious, weak-kneed, broken-winged Church institution. The Word, the Sacrament, and the Prayer must and will certainly not let themselves be imprisoned between the walls of churches and chapels. When the prayer for the Kingdom comes back again and ousts our self-centred prayers; when true Communion and true Baptism return; when the Word that is not ours comes upon us and to us, then we shall not only be amazed but horrified. Those who share in it will certainly not find their part cheap and easy to play. At all events the Church will cease to be a confined sphere of action. The Church will break out of its spell of yesterday. The community will once more become the salt of the earth and the light of the world. The Word will grow legs and walk to the end of the human world. A strange new spirit will flow from the Church, something akin to the spirit of adventure; a go-ahead spirit, a courageous, bold spirit of colonisation; indeed, we can quite boldly and openly call it a spirit of progress and world reform. When God's Word comes, and if it really is God's Word, then it will be heard again in the council chamber, it will be respected in

C

parliament, and the worlds of commerce and politics will either receive it with open arms or else set out to do battle with it.

I once knew a man who had his eccentricities like every other believer, but who was a true Christian. Among other things he thought in his early years that one had to grow a beard if one truly believed. He was the only man in the village who dared to grow a beard, which was perhaps in itself a kind of confession of faith. But for a long time he was also the only man in the village who defied all scorn and went bravely to Bible class, to which only women were in the habit of going. And it was he who as a young man brought the children of the village together at Sunday School. Nowadays the people of that district are very dependent on their bicycles in order to reach their fields, some of which are several miles apart; every growing child in that area rides a bicycle today because of the scattered nature of the work. Our bearded friend was the first man in the village to possess a bicycle, and he was laughed at when he rode it for the first time. Some hooligans stole it from him, and it was found two years later eaten with rust in a cess-pit. So the man with the beard had to suffer many provocations, for a pioneer spirit emanated from him; in spite of much persecution he did not let himself be discouraged. Strangely enough, in the course of the years this man was elected to various offices. When the village changed over from paraffin to electricity, the man with the beard became meter-reader and collector. He was made meat inspector of the village, a position which exposes a man to all kinds of corruption. In the course of his duties he visited every house and noticed how often in cattle transactions the small farmers in particular were cheated by dealers from other parts, who would lead them to believe that a piece weighed a certain amount, which was sometimes twenty or even fifty kilos too little. He saw that considerable loss was suffered in this way, especially by the more timid farmers. So this man took the initiative, and insisted that the village should acquire a public cattle-weighing machine, in spite of the fact that it was the smallest village for miles around and many bigger places were still a long way from thinking of such a thing. Consequently even the smallest farmer was able to weigh his cattle before selling them. When it came to finding someone trustworthy to take on the job of weighing officer, who had to ensure that the weighing was done accurately and that the scales were always true, then the village chose our man with the beard.

That is what faith in the Kingdom is: faith that reaches into everyday life, even as far as cattle-weighing machines. How many scales are not true, both at home and in the world; and how urgently the world needs men and women who will be responsible to God to see that justice is done, and that the helpless are not taken advantage of, and that the scales are true! That is what we meant when we said that in this second petition of the Lord's Prayer the essential thing is faith.

One day however the One will come who will weigh justly. One scale will contain eternal corruption, and the other faith and only faith. The dead will rise from their graves and, to use the words of that child, the Devil will die. Then the Son will give the Kingdom back to the Father; and to all who have believed, God will be all in all. And this is the ultimate perfection that we envisage when we pray, "Thy kingdom come".

The Will

THE third petition of the Lord's Prayer cost the life of Him who taught us to pray; for as we have already seen in the first two petitions, God's Will is to call this earth His own, it is to be His Kingdom, and He wants to rule it; it is to recognise in Him its one and only Lord, it is to give Him the glory, and to hallow His name. But if He wants to possess and rule this earth—and that is indeed His Will and His purpose for us—then first of all He must seek it again, for it has gone astray, it has lost touch with Him; first of all He must save this earth, for it is lost. But then that is exactly what He wants, that is His Will for this earth: His Will is to save. God does not want anyone to be lost, not even the least child, and He wants all people to have help. And if some one prays, "Thy will be done", then it can only mean one thing: "God in Heaven, save this earth; do not allow humanity to be lost, send the help that Thou hast promised us; may Thy will be done on earth as it is in Heaven".

And Jesus knows that the Father's way of seeking the earth and helping it and saving it is to send the Son. It is the Will of God for this earth that it should be sought through Jesus Christ, that it should experience God's help through Christ, and that through Him it should be saved. And although Christ knows that the Father's Will to save will lead Him into the deepest suffering, although He knows that for Him God's Will means the Cross, humiliation, and death, yet He teaches His own to pray: "Thy will be done". Certainly He recoils from the way along which the Father's Will is going to lead Him; but strangely enough, He teaches

His disciples to pray for the fulfilment of that same Will. And in the end, when the terrible path that the Father's Will has decreed for Him comes very near, He trembles and falters; but even then He still expects His disciples not to sleep but to watch and pray with Him; that is to say, they ought to have prayed with Him for the fulfilment of the Father's Will: they could not do it, but He could. If God's Will is that the earth should be saved in this most incomprehensible of all ways, then "Thy will be done".

The Will of God has actually already been done here on earth, because Christ showed His obedience in Gethsemane and on the hill of Golgotha; man has been helped by Him, and in Him the world has been saved. Therefore if we still pray for God's Will to be done on earth, it cannot now imply that it has not been done already, or that the work of salvation has not been successful, or that the Cross of Christ is not quite enough after all. No, it has been successful; there is no need for anything extra; it is enough in itself. But when in spite of this we still pray for God's will to be done here, our only concern can be that Christ's all-sufficient work of salvation should take effect throughout the whole world, and that the name of Christ should be known and confessed by all nations, and that all men should come to recognise their salvation. In this way the Will of God will be done "on earth as it is in heaven". That is to say, in Heaven Christ's work of salvation is already known and acknowledged. The whole of Heaven rejoiced as soon as Christ became a man and entered our poor flesh and blood, so how great the rejoicing there must have been at His words in Gethsemane: "Thy will be done" (Mt. XXVI.42). So the angels in Heaven are already ministering spirits of Christ, the eternal King. What matters now is that what happened there should also happen on earth: the important thing is that earth should become as subject to Christ the King as Heaven is already, in other words: "Thy will be done on earth as it is in heaven".

Now there is one aspect of this petition that is very strange: it would be perfectly acceptable to us straight away if only it had not to be understood in the way that I have just demonstrated, and if it were simply a matter of the Will of God being done on earth somehow or other. Who would not like that? One way or another this sort of thing would be desirable to all of us. Anyone who did not ardently long for it would be mad. It appeals to even the most selfish of us, for it is definitely much nicer to live in an earth ruled by God almighty than on an earth where all kinds of devilry are loose. And it is much more pleasant to dwell in an earth that is a garden of God and a Heaven on earth, so to speak, than in an earth that is a playground for new bombs, which it looks as if it is going to be. No, it goes without saying that God's Will should be done on earth in the general sense that the earth ought to be a decent place. It is unpleasant and burdensome to people that God's Will on earth should not only be a general Will to rule but a Will to save as well, a Will for our salvation; and that God's Will to save should be so closely bound up with the person of Christ, and that it leads along such a narrow way and through such a narrow gate. Just as that general Will of God almighty is attractive to us all, so this particular Will of God to save is unattractive and even irksome to us.

For this particular Will of God to save comes uncomfortably close to us: to put it mildly, it is expecting a lot to ask us to confess that we need to be saved, and the whole world, which naturally includes us, is lost without God's Will to save and the coming of Christ. So each one of us personally is touched on the raw by this Will of God to save, especially because we all have a kind of primitive other man in us, so to speak, and that is our self-will. It is well aware that it is fatally threatened by God's Will to save. Our self-will, quite rightly, scents a dangerous rival. For if we are in such a state that God has to save us, then that is a bad testimonial for our own will. And if God has to go as far as to send Christ to the Cross; if this way has become unavoidably necessary, then certainly things must have reached a stage where we could not save ourselves. This makes it clear to what a great extent the prayer that God's Will may be done, seen from our point of view, is in reality a call for help, a cry of direst need for God to hasten to our assistance, to save us, and to take pity on us personally. Consequently this petition is only prayed when self-will has collapsed and a prodigal son returns home to throw himself into the Father's saving arms. So in a certain sense this request costs the life of everyone who makes it: it demands our surrender and capitulation to Christ, and deals a deadly blow at the very heart of our self-will. That must be what Luther meant when he said that this was a "fearful prayer". We may well fear it! But rather that than ignorant babbling! If we had any inkling that we were praying for our personal surrender to Christ, then the words of this third petition would stick in our throats and we should find it hard to go on.

This third petition of the Lord's Prayer proves particularly unattractive and uncomfortable to good people—and which of us is not a good person? The world is swarming with people who "only meant it for the best". We are all full of good intentions; not a single one of us "wanted the war". In this town of ours, too, there are far more good people than you would suspect. No, that is not meant ironically; we have a long list of good and generally useful works in this town. We need only think of the new building that has been open to the public this past week. It is a good building: it is good partly because of the employment it has provided—an army of workmen and labourers has earned its bread by it for a good year now. But above all it is good because of its purpose. Is it not a sign of the noblest humanity that it is not a multiple store, nor a barracks, nor a bank, nor a sports stadium that towers up above this town, but that the skyline is dominated by a hospital? The fact that quite a small community has provided two and a half million pounds for its sick—that is £3750 per bed—demonstrates that there is money available for more than just guns and defences: even in these days £3750 can be found for a hospital bed. That is good; and it is not true that men can be enlisted only for evil causes: the facts contradict assertions of this kind. Even after this war no doubt many good things will be organised and undertaken. Perhaps a current of goodwill may even pass through the world; great things may be done for the poor, the old, and the children. In all our good will we men demand only one condition, and that is that our self-will must have its way and must not be thwarted. Thus the goodness with which the world is filled is wilful goodness, that is goodness partly without, partly directly contrary to the will of God to save, goodness of our own making. Is it no use at all then in the last resort? Is this world then sinking deeper and deeper into wickedness and farther and farther from God in spite of all our efforts for good? Can it be that all our efforts for good are in the end a visible expression of a particularly deep-seated and radical disobedience? Does it not strike you that all our good works have to be reasonable according to our reason, sensible after our sense, and practical and useful judged by our standards of usefulness? Do we not find again and again that in the end all these so rational good works are motivated by the unconscious but often also fully conscious claim to self-redemption? And does it not ultimately help and save at all, then? When all is said and done, has this generation set out to prove to God that man can help himself without Christ, and that therefore it was not at all urgent, indeed not even necessary to send Christ into the world and let Him suffer and die?

Yet salvation is not to be found where human wilfulness wants it, or thinks it should be, but where God wants it, there on the sinners' Cross. However, God's Will does not as a rule seem at all reasonable to people, not at all sensible, nor practical, nor useful. It was incomprehensible that Christ should die when He was only thirty years of age and had only just begun His ministry. The way from Gethsemane to Golgotha is incomprehensible, but it is God's way of salvation, the way chosen by Him to help men. What appears useless to us is precisely what in God's opinion was to prove most useful to humanity; what seems a loss to us is precisely what He turned into a gain. What seems folly to us God made into wisdom, and what remains for ever concealed to the wise and clever He has revealed to the innocent. What to men looks like a way of death has become the Way of Life, and where man's understanding can see nothing but defeat is the very place where victory is found. Where we see Christ captive, freedom is found; where we see a man helpless, help is found; and where we can see only a man powerless, there on the Cross the omnipotence of God is found. The Will of God which brings about salvation is as obscure and inconceivable as that, and it is this Will and not ours that is meant when we are exhorted to pray: "Thy will be done on earth as it is in heaven".

What effect does it have when a man really does renounce his self-will before the Cross? Does he not become very uninteresting as a result, and above all does he not lose his self-reliance when he loses his own will? Certainly if our human will is broken by people or circumstances we are usually left lying helpless; when some misfortune breaks us, then we are done for; when a crushing sorrow overwhelms us, then we are bowed and broken. It can happen that a strong personality, such as a schoolmaster or leader in some field or other, has such an effect on people that they lose themselves in him and stop being themselves. How many imitators are broken spirits as far as effective action is concerned! A father can break the spirit of his own children in this way, so that they are ineffectual and inhibited their whole life long. But strangely enough, and this is something that reason cannot understand, that does not happen with Christ. If we give up our self-will to Christ we find that our will is not completely destroyed or crippled, for our surrender to Christ is usually followed by the gift of freedom. The man who loses himself to people or things is lost; but the man who loses himself to Christ and His cause wins himself back, so to speak. Christ does not destroy our reason, our spirit, and our will: he takes them into His service and develops them, so that the will appears in a light that we would never have dreamed possible.

But when the Will of Christ, this higher Will, takes possession of a man and uses him as a tool, and when we discover that Christ does not destroy our will but renews it and makes use of it, then things might happen that are even more unwelcome to our flesh than ever. Difficulties might crop up in our lives which we had been completely unaware of earlier. Therefore our self-will, not unjustifiably has every reason to have a kind of secret fear of becoming a tool in the hand of Christ. It is just because Christ takes hold of us in this Lordly way that our flesh is so afraid: we feel like a man who does not know how to drive a motor car, but who has to sit at the wheel, turn on the ignition, and let in the clutch without knowing, once the engine is running, where the car is going to take him. But we must not be afraid when the Lord takes hold of us for, after all, we know where we are being taken, and even if the path goes up hill and down dale, over precipices and through narrow places, even if we are led through the valley of the shadow of death, yet the path leads us to salvation; for the Will of God under all circumstances is a saving Will! And although it is "a fearful thing to fall into the hands of the living God" (Heb. x.3), nevertheless it is for salvation.

Therefore, let Thy Will be wholly and completely

done. Our plight today consists in the fact that through
fear of God's whole Will we prefer, so to speak, to "go
halves" with God time and again. It is as if we needed
somehow or other to insure ourselves against God's Will.
So we can divide ourselves into two or even three parts:
we perhaps allow God to penetrate into our reason and our
minds, but we are not prepared to give up our will to Him;
that we want to keep to ourselves. As a result we have that
lukewarm Christianity, that mediocre, half or two-thirds
Christianity that is only too familiar to us. That is what
Christianity is suffering from. That is why it is so urgent
to pray: "Thy will be done, not half-heartedly but completely". The art of going halves can be exercised in other
ways too. One of the most popular is to set aside definite
places or times within which we allow God's will a certain
limited effectiveness. Churches and other sacred places
may be reserved for God, and we have achieved not a little
if we have set Sunday aside for Him. But what about
Monday? What would come of it if I, a shopkeeper by
trade, were to approach Monday clothed with the Will of
God? All sorts of unusual things would no doubt happen!
Or what if I as a councillor, instead of leaving it at home as
a private matter, were to go to the town hall accompanied
by the Will of God? What if I were to become a member
of Parliament, and the Will of God, instead of staying at
home or in the church pew, were to begin to participate
in the sittings? Or what if the Will of God were to
enter my calling of minister, whatever would come of
it! Would our flesh not be appalled at the very
thought?

And yet it is no less than that that we ask when we
pray, "Thy will be done on earth as it is in heaven", even
if it means having to follow the road that we are shown in
Matthew: "While he was still speaking to the people,
behold, his mother and his brothers stood outside, asking
to speak to him. But he replied to the man who told him,

'Who is my mother, and who are my brothers? . . . Whoever does the will of my Father in heaven is my brother, and sister, and mother' " (Mt. XII.46-50). It may happen that tax-collectors and fishermen become His heirs. But it could also happen—and what a tragedy it would be—that the pious and the good continually go halves and never come into their inheritance. Christ describes this possibility in the following words: " 'What do you think? A man had two sons; and he went to the first and said, "Son, go and work in the vineyard today". And he answered, "I will not"; but afterward he repented and went. And he went to the second and said the same; and he answered, "I go, sir", but did not go. Which of the two did the will of his father? They said, the first. Jesus said to them, Truly, I say to you, the tax collectors and the harlots go into the kingdom of God before you. For John came to you in the way of righteousness, and you did not believe him, but the tax collectors and the harlots believed him; and even when you saw it, you did not afterward repent and believe him' " (Mt. XXI.28-32).

Thy Will be done! If through the Holy Spirit we begin to bring this third petition of the Lord's Prayer before God in all honesty and sincerity, then what we are really saying amounts to this: "Lord, give freely of the miracle of inheritance in Thy Church, but let there be no more half-measures and half-heartedness".

Our Bread

Give us this day our daily bread . . .

IN the middle of the Prayer that Christ has taught His community we find the petition for our daily bread. Nowadays it probably strikes us as strange that many theologians of the past considered it quite unthinkable that the Lord could have been referring to ordinary bread. Whether this attitude is influenced by the ancient idea that all natural things are ugly and shameful—*naturalia turpia sunt!*—we do not know: the fact remains nevertheless that the majority of Christian commentators even to this day find it difficult to take this petition literally and not to force a spiritual meaning upon it as a matter of course. They regard it as lacking in spirituality, as too material and therefore too commonplace. Of recent years, however, the Church has been coming to realise that fear and abhorrence of natural and material things is not justified by the Bible. On the contrary it is right and proper to counter this false outlook of hyper-spirituality by pointing out that according to the testimony of the Scriptures there is not only a Godless but also a godly or holy kind of materialism in the sense that God does not despise and scorn material things but recognises them as His creation. God does not flee material things, but rather seeks them out in order to dwell in them, to redeem and rule them.

We find an instance of this holy materialism when Christ says to His disciples: "When you pray, go into your room and shut the door" (Mt. vi.6), if we understand that He most probably meant the larder, for we know for a fact that in most Israelite houses there was no room that could be shut up except the larder. Christ sends the man who wants to pray into the very place where all kinds of natural smells and odours hang in the air, where the empty jars remind the poor man of his poverty, and where the rich man is put in mind of poverty by the full jars. We encounter this godly materialism on almost every page of the Old Testament, so it is difficult to refer to isolated passages without quoting whole chapters. Nevertheless let us cite one example. In the book of the shepherd prophet, Amos of Tekoa, we read the words: "Thus says the Lord: 'For three transgressions of Israel, and for four, I will not revoke the punishment; because they sell the righteous for silver, and the needy for a pair of shoes' " (Am. II.6). God in the highest takes the trouble to find out where the poor man's greatest material need lies. God in His holiness knows exactly what the widow meant when she used to tell her children that she felt rising prices most in the higher cost of leather and the price of shoes. God bends so low into our petty and unattractive everyday affairs that He even finds out the price of a pair of shoes, a pair of shoes worn by a poor citizen of the earth as he treads the dust here below. But the New Testament, from beginning to end, consists in the fact that God, in Jesus Christ, assumed material form: "The Word became flesh and dwelt among us" (Jn 1.14). There where the world is at its worldliest, there where the earth is most earthly, so to speak, it pleases God to enter this time and world. Through the incarnation of Christ the social problem, the problem of food, has become God's problem. God takes our bodies seriously; they cannot be taken more seriously than that God Himself should assume a body and come down to our level where hunger, cold, and thirst abound. Through the incarnation of Christ we know that He really does mean bread when He teaches His own to pray, "Give us this day our daily bread", that is to say: give us food and clothing, a roof over our heads and whatever else our bodies need; give us work, health, freedom, and a native land; give us a life without constant fear, and let there be respect for human dignity among men—"Give us this day our daily bread".

Not only the bread itself but the very petition for bread is a divine favour. The very fact that we are allowed to ask for our daily bread is a divine gift of decisive importance in our lives. Yes, it is a case of being allowed to; the Christian is allowed to pray: "Give us this day our daily bread". When God makes the pressing needs of life the subject of a prayer, then He is transforming anxiety into trust in God. Fortunate the man who can know and trust that God the Father has bread to give; for God would not teach us to ask Him for it if He had none, or if He had not enough and to spare. Suppose that everybody were to begin to ask Him for bread now, would it not be for Heaven as if all the inhabitants of a town were to stream into the shops for food, with the result that the proprietors had to announce after a few hours that they were sold out, and had to shut up shop before closing time for lack of goods? Far from it: even if the whole world were to begin to ask; even if all the inhabitants of the earth were to stream in upon God our Father in Heaven, He would not have to "shut up shop" for lack of goods; the stream of God has water in abundance, and all the Father's servants have "bread enough and to spare". Even if all the prodigal sons the world over were to return home on the same day, that would not put the Father in an embarrassing position. We have a rich Father. It is this knowledge that makes us so happy when we pray this fourth petition of the Lord's Prayer. There is no fear that any one might go hungry or be cold because God has not enough food and warmth for all His children. He has plenty for every one.

So God's reason for giving us this petition is to relieve us of our fear and anxiety. It is His way of saying to us: "O you foolish children of men, why are you worried? Why will you not believe that I am capable of feeding and clothing you all? For each one of you I have more than a simple meal; a banquet awaits every one who comes home". But instead of considering our situation and trusting in God and turning back as one body we remain far away, estranged from the Father. In consequence, abundance and plenty are replaced by want and hunger. In other words God is having the same difficulty as various governments had during the war. They knew that there was enough for everybody, but so often people did not believe them, and in no time panic spread everywhere. Now fear reigned in place of trust. Driven by this fear some people bought twice, three times, or even ten times as much as they could possibly need, with the result that there was suddenly not enough for everybody. Then rationing had to be introduced, and once more there was enough to go round. That is God's situation with regard to us men. Fear drives us to provide for ourselves for ten, fifty, or even two hundred years in a most ridiculous way; in other words we are providing for a time when our teeth will have stopped giving trouble for a long time, and when we shall long ago have given up eating. Fear is so foolishly insatiable. It leads to shortage, anxiety, envy, and war, and the prayer for existence becomes the struggle for existence. Hunger, plague, crime, and all the rest of the horrors—how well we know the end of the story!

But God does not give up; God bids us pray, "Give us this day our daily bread". We are not only *allowed* to, as we have seen; we *have* to pray: He commands us to do it. By causing Christ to become a man God became irrevocably involved in the problem of bread; He became part of our everyday, material lives. God wants to be the provider of all things. He wants to have a hand in everything; He wants to be present, but within and not above. God has not such dainty hands as the farmer's daughter I saw the other day who put gloves on to fill a basket with firewood. If God needed gloves, then Christ would not have become a man. God touches this world, and in it He puts His hand to the plough without gloves. God wants to have a hand in everything that happens between the sowing and the harvest, so that the harvest will not be ruined by men's fear. God wants to have a hand in everything that happens between production and consumption; He wants to be a kind of built-in resistance in the electrical sense, so that the fatal currents and powerful blows of our wicked ways cannot play havoc with what is His. In all our doings and dealings God wants to have a regulating and distributive hand. The man who earnestly prays for his daily bread is thereby invoking the intervention of the almighty hand of God.

But let us make no mistake about the consequences of this divine intervention. The man who seriously prays for bread wants to see material results in this world.

The first effective result of this petition is that whoever prays seriously learns that what is usually called "private property" and what we understand by "private property" has no place in the Holy Scriptures. Admittedly the conception of property is not done away with, but this rigid, narrow conception of property is continually subjected to a beneficial and most necessary process of loosening and softening. For the man who prays for his daily bread knows that everything he has is bestowed on him as a gift and belongs to him only as such. The Roman law of private property was heathen in spirit. Strictly speaking there is no such thing in the Bible, where all property is held in trust. From the point of view of the Bible we men are not actual possessors, but tenants and trustees of all that we have and are. Someone else is the owner. The earth is the Lord's, and everything in it, silver and gold, is His; we are responsible to him for it, but we cannot dispose of one single penny as we please, for it is a gift from God. This is that peculiar Christian responsibility for everything earthly, which leads to faithfulness in the least of things. People of today have a sense of responsibility too: it would be wrong

D

to speak of the modern European as an irresponsible person. But this responsibility is something material and worldly. The man in the street thinks he "owes it to himself" or to his children or to humanity or to some circumstances of time or situation. The Holy Scriptures however make us responsible to God for all our doings and dealings, they subject us to the greatest and ultimate responsibility.

The second effective result of this fourth petition of the Lord's Prayer is economic dependence on God. The man who seriously prays for his daily bread knows the secret of privation and plenty. The fact that men have to earn their bread makes them more dependent than anything else in the world, dependent on men, governments, and things. How enslaved man is by economic dependence on others! How horribly true is the cynical saying: "Whose bread I eat, his song I sing". But by giving us this fourth petition of the Lord's Prayer God wants to draw us into dependence on Him and Him alone, and by so doing wants to give us a little freedom and independence from earthly powers and principalities which so often appear to us in the form of earthly providers of bread. The man who can pray for bread knows the truth of the Psalmist's words: "These all look to thee, to give them their food in due season . . . when thou openest thy hand, they are filled with good things". He also knows how seriously the following verse is to be taken: "When thou hidest thy face, they are dismayed; when thou takest away their breath, they die and return to their dust" (Ps. CIV.27-9). God can open His hand and close it, God can bless and curse, and can even change curse into blessing and blessing into curse: it is all in His power. The Christian is utterly dependent upon God. This introduces a new kind of discipline: the spiritual discipline that a man experiences when he begins to realise that everything is dependent on God's blessing. So at times the prayer for bread can have a chastening effect. This puts me in mind of a story I shall never forget. In the

winter of 1905 a cheese merchant was buying up the stock
of a widow with six children just after the sudden death of
her husband. Taking advantage of the helpless widow's
circumstances he beat down the price until she let him have
the goods at a ridiculously low figure. Before the end of
the year this rich and respected man sent a registered letter
to the woman he had cheated, in which he said that his
conscience had been tormenting him throughout the year,
and that in addition he had had bad luck both in business
and family life, so that all the time he could not help
thinking of the injustice he had done to that helpless widow
and her six fatherless children. The letter contained a
cheque repaying the money of which he had deprived her.
Thus experience of privation and plenty can discipline a
businessman so that he becomes God-fearing in his dealings.
Wherever this fourth petition of the Lord's Prayer is prayed
in all seriousness, the result can be economic dependence
upon God.

And then the third result. Asking for bread also implies
giving thanks for bread. The petition for bread leads us
into the mystery of thankfulness. The man who understands thankfulness ceases to be a glutton for good living.
The thankful man is contented and consequently always
has something left for others. The thankful man becomes a
giver. It is food for thought when a simple old Sunday
School teacher who has collected for many a good Church
cause in her day sums up her experience of collecting in the
drastic words: "Ladies in fur coats never liked giving". In
his personal modesty the man who has learned to be thankful
will always have an open hand and an open house. He will
spread a blessing that will extend not only to those nearest
to him, but also to those farthest away, even to the ends of
the earth. Active gratitude is the third effect of the petition
for bread.

When this petition is prayed in such a way as to weaken
our conception of property, subject us to ultimate

dependence on God, and lead us into gratitude, then there is enough for everyone; then there is no one who lacks anything, and hunger has no longer any place. But instead of this a monstrous thing has happened: God who quite unmistakably became part of our material life, has been pushed out again. We did not want Him there; we did not want Him to have a hand in it; we suggested that He should spare Himself and asked Him to refrain from defiling His hands with our dirt. In actual fact, however, we wanted to be left alone to carry on our business without God. But God wants to defile Himself; God does not accept the dispensation from the office of material supplier that we offer Him, for it was not for nothing that God became man in Jesus Christ. God wants to have a place in all humanity, in everything to do with men. God wants to be the built-in resistance and at the same time the established mediator. That is why He taught Christianity to pray, "Give us this day our daily bread".

Sometimes we are beset by the secret fear that it is too late for our generation to turn back from its estrangement from God, and that the distance between God and our Godless materialism which is a law unto itself has grown too great for the two, God and our everyday lives, ever to come together again. We are afraid that the gap has become far too wide and that people have grown far too accustomed to it. From a human point of view this is no doubt a justifiable fear. If we look back along the way which we have come, then we might well despair at the distance. But in God's eyes there simply is no distance that is too great or insuperable for Him. Since we know that He overcame the greatest gap of all and covered the greatest distance of all, that between Heaven and earth, we can make this petition which incorporates both God and our bread with new hope and new trust.

And in conclusion, this prayer is of a spiritual nature too, of course; for as we have seen, behind all bread can be

discerned the spirit which either has power over bread
where we are responsible and grateful, or, where we are
masterless, takes the authority upon itself. A farmer I
know in the Emmental uses this form of grace at table every
day: "Lord, we give thee praise and thanks for this holy
food and drink, for these holy gifts, favours, and blessings.
Lord who livest and reignest as a true God be glorified for
ever. Amen". But this same prayer is found in an old
Communion liturgy. It has found its way from the Communion table in the church to the dining table in a farmer's
kitchen. We are reminded that God has prepared a table
in the midst of the nations and has said, "I am the bread".

Our Debts

And forgive us our debts, as we also have forgiven our debtors . . .

DIFFICULT though it is for us to grasp, it is gradually beginning to dawn on us that the world in which we live is in the process of collapsing. The destroyed houses, villages, and towns are not only isolated accidents or chance setbacks, but signs of a collapse. And it is striking that today, particularly in conversation with uncomplicated people, we are always hearing that things must change now, and that the world must under no circumstances go back to where it was before. Certainly it must not! The slightest step in the old direction leads to a precipice. The world is once more due for a radical turn-about or for a collapse.

There is a certain unanimity in the conviction that things must change now. This verdict is beginning to be accepted by public opinion as being for the general good. But how things are to change, and where they are to change, and by what means the change is to take place—there is no general agreement about that. Of course there are many people who think they know exactly what must change and where the change must take place, and how and when and above all by whom the change is to be brought about. But the views are so varied, and there are so many proposals and divergent opinions that even at this stage there are many opposing camps. And the different views are at war with one another, and so they bring us back to a state of distress once more.

For all their diversity, these proposals for reform resemble one another very closely in that they are aimed only at one particular aspect of the trouble, so that in the final analysis these proposals are merely part processes or plans for repair. At times, admittedly, mending is a good thing: we learned that in the years of growing shortage of materials. Many a man began to go about with patched trousers again, and many a woman had to make up her mind to make something new out of something old. But the time always comes when you cannot mend any more, because the old has become rotten and decayed, and stitches, nails, and rivets have nothing left to grip on to. And there also comes the day, not only in the case of shoes, clothes, and tools, but also in the relationships between people, when the truth of the Lord's words is demonstrated, that you cannot put a new piece of cloth on an old garment, and when it becomes necessary to put new wine into new bottles. At times like this it is obvious that what is at stake is not only a part but the whole. It seems to me that the time has come when the world is not only in need of repair but in need of renewal, and when it can no longer be helped by any number of well-intentioned reforms but only by a reformation of the head and the limbs.

But it is not only we men who are concerned about the state of the world; it is not only we who are aware of the threatening course of events; it is not only we who are anxious about what might happen, and what changes ought to take place: someone else was concerned long before we were; someone else was worried about the world long ago and, long before we were aware of it, noticed where the fault lay. God sees it: He saw it long ago and said where the trouble was, and His opinion, it seems to me, is decisive. He said that the fundamental trouble is that we men are sinful. Sin is the greatest evil, and sin means that we have deserted God, and that instead of obeying Him we have cut ourselves off and estranged ourselves from Him. Indeed God does not only say that sin is the greatest evil, but that the real evil in fact is our sinning. That is what God thinks, and that is what He says.

But besides saying where the trouble lies God also points
to the remedy. The remedy is forgiveness; that is what we
read in the Bible. It is so simple that time and again it is
too simple for men: they look for complexities and get
further and further from the goal. Consequently they miss
the point both in where the fault lies and in where the
remedy lies. That was the simple discovery that the
Reformers of the sixteenth century made: they recognised
the one thing that was needful; they saw both the trouble
—that we men are sinful—and the cure—that God forgives.
Their age, like today, was a time of sensational discoveries
and inventions. Not the atomic bomb but gunpowder
had been invented; America had been discovered; and
printing was in its early stages. And in the midst of that
busy and sensational age a handful of men made the strangely
quiet discovery that the fault lay not in this or that, but in
the hearts of men, and that the remedy was not discoveries
and inventions, but the forgiveness of sin. And this discovery—it was only a re-discovery after all—became
strength in weakness, a city set on a hill and a light in darkness. Men began to have hope once more and drew new
vitality from this truly epoch-making discovery. Yes, it
was just this apparently quietest petition of the Lord's
Prayer that made world history. How true are Nietzsche's
words: "It is the quietest words that bring the storm.
Thoughts that come on tip-toe move the world". Therefore we would do well to give this quietest of all petitions
our particular attention.

It does not stand alone in the Lord's Prayer: it is one
of the seven petitions, with several others before and after
it; but of all of them it is *the* petition, the central one, the
kernel of the Prayer. Even grammatically it is connected
like no other with the petitions before and after it. Notice
the striking "and"! God has linked up the prayer for
forgiveness and the prayer for bread with a special "and".
The ancient text distinctly uses the word "*kai*". Give us

our daily bread *and* forgive us our debts. This "and" must
not be overlooked. It is obviously being demonstrated to
us by this arrangement of the individual petitions that
bread and sin belong together in a particular way, that our
struggle for bread and our anxiety about it cause us men to
sin against one another more than anything else. Because
sin is of a social character, so to speak, every word that we
have said about the petition for bread also cries out for
the forgiveness of sin. So it was not by accident that our
consideration of the fourth petition of the Lord's Prayer
finally led us to the Communion table. But this word
"and" is instructive and important for yet another reason.
God evidently wants to tell us that man needs both bread
for his stomach, because without it he will die, and, more
important still, he needs forgiveness for his soul, for without
it he will also die; he will die twice over, not only physically
but also spiritually; he will not only die in the temporal
world but also for eternity. In one respect, however, the
stomach is better off: it has a stronger voice, so to speak,
for it grumbles if it does not get bread; it has been given the
warning voice of the watchdog. The soul, however, has
a softer voice and therefore often goes unheard. The soul
does not grumble; it can only sigh. This sighing must not
go unheard. Man lives by bread, it is true. But as well
as the holy kind of materialism there is an unholy and un-
godly kind which tries to persuade us that man lives by
bread alone. But this is refuted by the Prayer that the
Lord taught us. We are told in no uncertain manner that
man does not live by bread alone, but by every single
word that comes from the lips of God. And the most
important word that comes from the lips of God is forgiveness. Therefore: "Give us this day our daily bread;
and forgive us our debts, as we also have forgiven our
debtors".

Doubts have also been raised about the order in which
these two petitions are placed. To some people it would

seem more logical if the prayer for forgiveness had been
put before the petition for bread because, after all, the
former is by far the more important: it is the central
petition. But the order in which the Lord taught His
community is well founded; He is well aware of His reason
for putting the petition for bread first. God is remarkably
generous in these things; He does not bargain as we narrow-
minded men are in the habit of doing, for instance when
we will only help those poor who are connected with us
through membership of the same party or church. God
gives bread even before a man is prepared to accept forgiveness from Him. God sends down rain upon the good and
the evil, and lets His sun shine on the just and the unjust.
He feeds many a scoundrel, but He does not regret it. What
truly kingly generosity! But this order, which means
simply that God does not indulge in bargaining because
His grace is free, must not be misunderstood. And we
should be doing so if we were to deduce from it that the
petition for bread was the more important. As if God
could not place the less important thing first for once!
A few weeks ago a well-turned-out speaker, who evidently
worshipped the godless kind of materialism, was addressing
a public meeting. He said that he could not understand
why Christians constantly go on about sin and forgiveness,
as if they had nothing more urgent to say. He followed this
up with the impassioned plea: "Give everyone bread and
you'll have paradise on earth, and all your problems will
be resolved at one stroke". This smart solution was greeted
with many approving nods. But we cannot help asking,
"Is that true?" He was perhaps not wrong if he meant
that in a predominantly unsocial age the Church had largely
forgotten the petition for bread, and thought that it could
preach to empty stomachs. But he *was* wrong if he
intended to push the question of bread to the forefront,
and to belittle and put aside the question of sin. If everyone
had bread the world might well become a fools' paradise,

probably, alas, a very sinful one at that. But a true paradise? Every schoolboy today knows that if we are to exist at all, then bread must be supplemented at least by games as the minimum spiritual requirement for existence, so to speak, or, as Dostoevsky's Grand Inquisitor says, by miracles. O no, the fact that we have bread by no means guarantees us paradise on earth. But on the other hand, the fact that we had forgiveness, although admittedly it would not bring paradise on earth (that would be saying too much!) would at least give a certain peace. It is not at all impossible to conceive that if all people had peace of soul through the forgiveness of their sin, then they would no longer hunger insatiably for more and more, and would stop piling sin upon sin in their greed. When the power of forgiveness gains ground, many social problems solve themselves. And while they remain unsolved they are indubitable proof that we lack forgiveness. I wonder what that man who scorned forgiveness of sin would have to say about a farmer who gave his cattle plenty to eat and drink every day but who neglected to clean out the cow shed for a week, or even six months, or a whole year? While enjoying a full drinking trough and an overflowing manger they would be rotting away in their own filth. Of course there are no such stupid farmers, or if there were, they would not be quite right in the head, but there are such stupid people. They think that they can go not only for a year, but for forty, sixty, or eighty years without being "cleaned out", in other words, without forgiveness of sin. We know quite well why we come together Sunday after Sunday and submit ourselves to the Word of mercy. Man lives by forgiveness, and a world without mercy perishes by its own filth and by its unforgiven sin, because it thinks it does not need to be "cleaned out". While enjoying a full manger—perhaps the state manger of the Soviet Union—while enjoying a full drinking trough—perhaps the golden trough of the U.S.A. —we can still perish miserably in our sin. That is why we have the connecting "and": "And forgive us our debts, as we also have forgiven our debtors".

But God has not only said where the trouble lies; He has not only said how it could be remedied, but—and here we are confronted with such a majestically splendid fact that we are helpless when we try to discuss it, and therefore I can only express it in the most simple language: God has helped us already. He was so deeply concerned about this world that He would not wait any longer. Christ said: "Your Father knows what you need before you ask him", and here we see the truth of His words. God forgave our sin before we could ask Him to. We can see how thorough and radical His attack on evil was in that He sacrificed His dearest and best, His Son. The renewal of the world took place under Pontius Pilate, and everything that has deserved the name of renewal since then points to and springs from the Cross where Christ died. That is the turning-point in the history of the world. Hardly anything can happen now that could have a more comprehensive and decisive significance for the solution of the social question than God's unique sacrifice fulfilled under Pontius Pilate. So the social turning-point, the turning-point in the history of the nations in fact, is that sacrifice which no man could make, that sacrifice which was necessary for the forgiveness of all sin. There is only one thing in this world that is greater than our human sin, and that is God's sacrifice of atonement.

From now on the petition for forgiveness no longer means that God should provide forgiveness: it has already been provided; it is complete. No, from now on this petition is for us men a plea that we might recognise where the trouble lies, and how and where and when and through whom it has already been remedied. There are many senseless things in this world; our so-called cleverness is especially full of absurdities: but surely the most senseless thing of all is that while God's forgiveness is complete, the nations go on living as if it were not complete, and that since Christ was crucified whole generations still perish in the morass because they turn down God's sacrifice and refuse to accept forgiveness of their sin. It is downright madness that whole generations are suffering from unforgiven sin in spite of the fact that Christ died on the Cross for everyone. That is why we pray: "Lord, grant that more people, that many people, that all people may come to the recognition of their sin and thus to the recognition of merciful forgiveness".

Forgiveness is there, and it is offered to us. We have been allowed to say the words yet once more, and yet once more the table has been prepared for us. We can taste and see how good the Lord is; He has provided forgiveness for us. And the place for this, the place that is there for the express purpose of offering forgiveness, is the Church. But we are bound to ask: what is the Church's situation? Surely the Church contains the people who have heard and accepted the Word? After all, we have been baptised and go to Communion. We have forgiveness—but why does the world not see more evidence that there is a Church, a place where there is a Communion table and a baptismal font? The answer is that the forgiveness that is proferred is as yet not wholly accepted, and also that there is someone who understandably has no joy in forgiveness, but who, on the contrary, derives pleasure from accusing people: the accuser who accuses us day and night. Luther says that accusing is the true business of the Devil. And a dirty business too!

This accuser has two favourite manoeuvres designed to mislead us: one is directed at our own selves, the other at our fellow men. He succeeds time and again in showing us the immensity of our sin, and thus obscuring the magnitude of forgiveness. He constantly whispers to us to look to ourselves instead of looking to Christ and Him alone. These are just diversions, but because of them we Christians are always faint-hearted, and never dare to accept forgiveness and enjoy it and live by it. And so, instead of being joyful witnesses of forgiving grace we become such "lame ducks", such miserable, timorous, and handicapped half-Christians, that we are incapable of making the world envious and covetous of what we have experienced. And so the light is hidden under a bushel.

The second manoeuvre is of an even more perfidious nature and runs through the Church like a plague. Instead of giving others the benefit of forgiveness, we are misled by the accuser into taking an inordinate interest in the sins of others and noting their faults. Far too many Christians are interested in other people's sins. What a shameful amount of time we spend gossiping about other people's sins and criticising and mocking at them: we pass judgment on them as if there were not something more sensible and more pressing to do, namely to pass on the forgiveness that we ourselves have received. The sun cannot do other than shine; the birds are there to sing; the flowers must bloom; and fire must burn—and the purpose of forgiveness is forgiving. Forgiveness that does not forgive is not forgiveness. The light of the world and the salt of the earth are so little in evidence because we Christians are more interested in the sins of others than in the forgiveness which we should hand on. Yet we say, ". . . as we also have forgiven our debtors".

However forgiveness must not be regarded as a universal theory; it must be shown to be a practical reality in every individual case. It is all the more important that there should be a Church with light and salt to offer at a time when not only politics and economics, but all aspects of life, particularly accusation and condemnation, so easily acquire a collective form. It is this mass judgment that the Church has to oppose. Now the Jews are blamed for everything, now the Communists, or the Germans, and they in their turn may be relieved of responsibility by the capitalists. In the face of this kind of wholesale condemnation of humanity the Church must be deeply sincere when it prays, ". . . as we also have forgiven our debtors".

One Saturday evening some time ago I gave a talk to the men of a certain congregation in a room at an inn. Before I began, the chairman said to me, "That man sitting at the middle table is a German. There is quite a lot of talk about him at present because there is a court case proceeding against him, but he has not been found guilty. There might be a little trouble; we shall have to watch out. He is a bit of a bragger, but a harmless fellow really". And sure enough, when the general discussion started up after my talk, a man at the back of the room suddenly got up and shouted: "That fellow at the middle table must leave!" and as the German did not move, the other man called him by name and demanded that he should go at once. Thereupon some one else got up and said, "We may be in a room in an inn filled with tobacco smoke, but we are assembled as a Church. That man at the middle table is in church here, in other words in the place where forgiveness rules. The law-suit concerning our brother in faith is in the hands of the authorities, and will be properly examined by them. But that does not alter the fact that he is our brother in faith. Therefore he must not leave".

That is what church is. The accuser constantly calls to us who are in the church; "That man must leave!" Indeed, how often have we met people on the way to church and thought: "These people don't really belong in a church". Yes, the accuser even whispers in our own ears; "*You* must leave!" But Christ stands up against the accuser and says, "For the sake of the blood I shed you do not have to leave". You would have to leave if it were not for Christ. Which of us would not have to go if God were to stand up and judge? But the Table is prepared and we are all invited to stay.

Our Temptation

And lead us not into temptation . . .

"AND forgive us our debts, as we also have forgiven our debtors": this could actually be the end of the Lord's Prayer. At all events the most important and decisive part has been said. What more can one want than the forgiveness of all one's sins? What more can one need than the full grace of Christ? What gift from the hand of God could possibly be greater than forgiveness? But strangely enough the Prayer does not break off there; Christ descends abruptly to a lower plane and continues: "And lead us not into temptation". And once again we are struck by this significant "and", which we have come across before: "*And* lead us not into temptation".

This "and" joins the sixth petition of the Lord's Prayer to the preceding one just as a trailer is coupled to a heavy lorry. "And lead us not into temptation" is a kind of trailer to the preceding petition for forgiveness. And strictly speaking the sixth petition is also concerned with forgiveness and grace. We have not started on something new: the important thing now is that we should retain the forgiveness that we prayed for in the fifth petition, and indeed more than this: it is important that forgiveness, the greatest gift of Heaven, should now develop and take effect in the man who has received it, so that the gift of grace may bear fruit in patience. For the pardoned Christian leads a perilous existence. The man who has experienced grace, and whose petition for forgiveness has been heard must take great care, for now there is danger in delay. The early fathers of our Church divided all the enemies that lurk around the man

56

who is pardoned into three main groups. We shall simply
follow the fathers of our faith.

The first enemy comes from within: it is our own hearts,
where all temptation is centred. We have no excuse: that
is what James means when he says that no one should lay
the blame on God when he is tempted. Temptation begins
in our own hearts, because even if our sins have been
forgiven, unfortunately we do not stop being sinners: we
are not promoted to a sinless condition. Certainly we are
pardoned sinners, but still sinners nevertheless. It may be
an imperfect comparison, and one that may well be misunderstood, but forgiveness and sin make me think of
human nails and hair, which grow again when they have
been cut: indeed they grow particularly well and fast just
after being cut. And it is the same with sin: just after it has
been forgiven it tries to "grow again". Therefore let no
one think that he is over the bridge and that he has now
"won out" once and for all, for sin grows again. If you are
tempted to play the pious saved man, then take care, for soon
enough you will be up to the ears in sin again. You can
have a careless attitude to forgiveness. People sometimes
say that our Roman Catholic brothers in faith only go to
confession in order to go on sinning happily afterwards.
It may well be that the way in which forgiveness is offered
there is particularly open to temptation, and easily leads
itself to the misuse of forgiveness. This misuse does not
only threaten our neighbour; it lies in wait for everyone,
and no Christian is proof against it. It is easy for us to
get up from our knees in a casual frame of mind, or to
come out of Church or communion in a negligent and
perfunctory manner; in fact some people can go on sinning
carelessly on the strength of an advance payment of forgiveness. But a struggle awaits the man whose sins have been
forgiven, be he Roman Catholic or Protestant. That is
why Christ bids us not to stop short after the petition for forgiveness but to continue: "And lead us not into temptation".

E

In other words: Father, grant that we do not fall all the deeper while thinking that we are standing upright; grant that Thy gift of the assurance of salvation may not become for us the certainty of salvation; grant that we may remain watchful against sin; preserve us from the misuse of Thy forgiveness. Grant us all this; Thou must grant it, for we can certainly not keep ourselves from the careless use of the gift of forgiveness; we have to be protected. But of course God wants to protect us, for Christ certainly did not teach us this sixth petition of the Lord's Prayer in order to make fools of us, but in order to hear and answer our prayer. He wants to protect us from the worst of all possible dangers, the careless misuse of His forgiveness. To each and every one who seriously prays for it He grants that forgiveness will not become a habit or an empty mechanism; He grants that every day the plough of repentance will turn over the earth anew, and that every morning we shall experience the miracle of grace once again. God can and will grant this through the Holy Spirit. The Holy Spirit can prevent the misuse of grace. Thus the petition "and lead us not into temptation" is intrinsically closely bound up with the prayer for the Holy Spirit.

The second enemy, or rather the second group of enemies, does not come from within but from without, from our so-called environment. Opportunity does not only make the thief; opportunity makes sinners of every kind. There are occasions which particularly lend themselves to temptation and circumstances that are especially dangerous, when we can only pray and cry out, "and lead us not into temptation". Luther distinguishes between two kinds of temptation from without: those from the right and those from the left. There are various temptations from the left. We may perhaps fall into dire poverty; we may become seriously ill; we may experience difficulties in our married lives; we may be dogged by ill luck in our jobs; we may be slandered by other people; we may suffer one blow of fate after another: this is when temptation from the left assails us. We lose sight of God's grace; we are tempted to doubt God's goodness and mercy; and we can scarcely believe that in spite of everything we have God's grace and forgiveness. We must resist this kind of temptation, and the best way to resist it is to pray, "And lead us not into temptation", in other words, grant that I may be satisfied with Thy grace. The very prayer is resistance. But even worse is the temptation from the right: we may perhaps grow rich; we may be successful in our jobs; we may boast that we have never needed a doctor in our lives: this is the sort of continuous good luck that can become a source of danger not only for individuals but for whole nations too. Everyone may speak well of us, and we may gain recognition in our work: temptation from without strikes with particularly accurate, sharp, and telling blows, so that eventually we become arrogant or self-righteous, and in the end we even believe that we deserve our good fortune. This is the temptation from the right: we stop being grateful, and begin to savour the most splendid gifts both of this world and the world to come as if they were a foregone conclusion. But astonishingly enough we can resist this too by praying, "And lead us not into temptation".

The temptation from without can come very subtly too, slipping unnoticed through the air, as it were. One kind of temptation like this is the so-called atmosphere in which one lives. Every atmosphere encourages temptation to some extent or other: the more pleasant it is, the greater the temptation. Every country has its own atmosphere, and so has every town, just as the homes we grew up in had their special atmosphere. This tempting quality of the air has also been called "slow infiltration". In the years 1931–1935 I often had the opportunity of talking to a man who was a member of a group known as the Bruderhofleute (Hutterites). This group was persecuted, and had to flee from Germany, and found spiritual peace in South America. This man told me that when individual members of his society had revisited the Germany of that time for a few months and then gone abroad again, they were not a little dismayed to find how much they had been affected spiritually during this time: the Godless, anti-Christian atmosphere of that period had settled on their souls like a touch of mildew. Yes, they faced temptation over there in those days, unusually severe temptation. But some people managed to resist it. We on this side of the Rhine have never had to be prepared to sacrifice all we have for our faith: but in that Germany there were people who did. So in fact it is possible to resist the temptation of atmosphere and that slow infiltration. Christ furnished this resistance: it is the Word of God and the Holy Spirit. Through God's Word the Holy Spirit can expose the most cleverly hidden minefield and uncover the most cunningly concealed snare. The Holy Spirit opens men's eyes to invisible enemies too. Through the Holy Spirit the Word of God shines like a light in the darkness. The Holy Spirit makes the Word of God a weapon of resistance, the shield that blunts the poisoned arrows of the evil one, the helmet of salvation, the breast-plate of righteousness and the sword of the spirit. And it is this armour that we are asking for when we pray, "And lead us not into temptation"; and Christ will answer our prayer. He will not let His own be tempted beyond their powers of resistance.

And the third enemy comes not from within, from the heart, nor from without, from one's environment, but from below, out of the abyss. It is the Devil himself, who "prowls around like a roaring lion, seeking someone to devour" (1 Pet. v.8), and the Devil directs his attentions above all at the man who has been forgiven. What a great day it is when the doctor tells his patient that he can begin to get up for a little while now. But at the same time he raises a warning finger and adds, "Be careful". When you are beginning to get well, and can get up for a little, then be doubly careful, for then there is danger of embolism and of a relapse. What a great day it is when the governor of a prison can inform prisoner No. 98 that this day is the day of his release. But he too raises his finger and adds the warning: "Be careful; the day of release is doubly dangerous". But what a truly great day it is when a man can begin to rise from the sick-bed of sin and become convalescent. What a great day it is when fetters begin to loosen, when here and there a link of the chain weakens, and a bar of the prison of sin breaks. But be doubly careful then! It is true, as we know, that the angels in Heaven rejoice, so you too can join in the rejoicing. But there is someone who does not want to rejoice, and who stands aside and gnashes his teeth, "seeking someone to devour". When Christ was being prepared with the grace of the Holy Spirit for the office of Redeemer, the Spirit led Him straight from His baptism into the wilderness, so that He might be tempted by the Devil. Immediately after Judas had partaken of the Last Supper, the ball began to roll. And when the rest of the disciples got up from the great Supper which they were privileged to enjoy with their Lord on that Maundy Thursday evening, Christ knew that now Satan hungered for them, and that He must warn them: "Watch and pray . . . the spirit indeed is willing, but the flesh is weak" (Mt. xxvi.41). The Devil is like a cat. No cat will chase a dead mouse: it prefers live ones. The Devil does not pursue dead men or half-alive Christians: he hungers for living food. That is why every man who has been forgiven has particular reason to continue after the fifth petition of the Lord's Prayer with: "And lead us not into temptation".

But here in the struggle with the third enemy there is, astonishingly enough, not only protection, as in the struggle with sin in our own hearts; there is not only resistance, as in the conflict with the world: here in the struggle with the Devil there is even victory. For here Christ has conquered

once and for all.   Here He bore the brunt of all the cunning
onslaughts of the Devil, and held out to the end, and as
victor He won through to glory by way of the Cross and
through the grave.   Because the Devil has been defeated
the prayer: "And lead us not into temptation" is filled with
the hope of victory.   He is finished, however much he may
try to shake our assurance of salvation; however much he
may "accuse us day and night", the Holy Spirit proves to
our spirit that we are God's children.   We are sure of this
because Christ has stopped up the mouth of the accuser.
The fifth petition has been heard: no devil can ever change
that.   The help from above is stronger than the attack from
below.   It is fulfilled.

And one further observation.   It would be all too easy
in the case of this sixth petition of the Lord's Prayer to get
lost in all kinds of heights and depths, and for all our
discussion to miss the essential point, which is that we are
here concerned with forgiveness.   In our discussion of this
petition in particular we must therefore guard against
being distracted by these intricacies.   For instance people
have so often come to grief on the over-subtle question:
"Can God lead us into temptation: is such a thing per-
missible?"   As if there were anything that God cannot do
or is not allowed to do!   As if God had to ask our permission; as if we had the authority and the right to say what
He can and cannot do!   Certainly there is danger in thinking
that God cannot lead us into temptation, and that He can
only guide us; there is danger in praying merely for
guidance, and in narrow-mindedly expecting only guidance
from God.   Christ knew only too well why He did not
teach us to pray merely for guidance, but expressly: "And
lead us not into temptation".

Let us accept this petition quite simply as a gift!   We
ourselves would probably never have hit upon such a
prayer at all of our own accord: but He thought of it, and
surely He knows why.   Let us accept it as a special gift of

grace. And if reason objects, then we can counter it by asking: Are you not content with the fact that the Devil obviously does not have his own way with temptation, and that he is evidently not free? Are you not content and do you not give praise and thanks to God that in all the dark intrigues of the Devil you have been given a refuge in God, to whom you can pray because God has the last word and the Devil and his temptation are subject to the highest control?

One last refinement of temptation is still possible, and that is to be too stupid or too clever simply to accept the gift, and daily and earnestly to pray that God should not lead us into temptation.

Our Distress

But deliver us from evil . . .

SAVE us! This is the cry with which Christ ends the seven petitions of His Prayer. This call for help is remarkably urgent: it is more than urgent, it is desperate. It is reminiscent of the Psalmists. "Save us from evil" is the literal translation. But when we consider that Christ ends His Prayer with this cry of distress instead of on a note of harmony and satisfaction, then we tend to be a little embarrassed, for is it not true that our situation on the whole does not compel us to cry out, "Save us!"? There are a great many Christians among us who would not know what to make of a cry of this kind, who do not understand it at all, who are not in the picture, who would be acting falsely if they were suddenly to join in this cry, and to whom this sort of thing seems like a false alarm, because they are under the impression that things are not in such a bad way as to give them cause to cry out, "Save us from evil". True, each one of us has his own particular burden to bear; the shoe pinches every one of us somewhere or other. True, we are all in need of many things, some more than others. But when someone has to cry out, "Save us", then he no longer needs just this or that; he not only needs just many things, his need is so great that all he can do is cry out for help. True, we also have so many personal petitions: there are so many different things to pray for, and there is such a wide choice for our prayers. But the man who prays the seventh petition of the Lord's Prayer has no choice left, because he knows that he is doomed unless he is saved: if he prays this petition, then he must be at the end of his tether. That is why this seventh petition strikes us as

64

remarkably "unrespectable": it is the petition of the down and out who needs to be saved. We feel that this petition was spoken and offered to Christians whose danger was vastly different from ours today, who were differently placed in relation to authorities, principalities, and powers; who were deprived of their civic dignity, and whose very property and lives were in danger; Christians who had so many and such professed enemies and opponents that they could do nothing but cry out, "Save us! Cut short our time of misery, deliver us from evil!"

In our present condition we are almost a little ashamed of this petition. It is as if a curtain were drawn aside revealing to us a need for deliverance in relation to which we are orphan children. Indeed it is only to be expected that this petition will not only make us feel ashamed, but will probably irritate us, the more we understand it. We might be irritated that Christ really had nothing else to offer to His Church in the end but the prospect of a situation which might become so serious that we would be bound to cry out, "Save us! Deliver us from evil!" Among Christians in particular there are many who secretly or openly cherish the view that if one believes, then things must go well for one, or even better than for others. But now when Christ ends His series of petitions with a decided call for help, this seventh petition in all its unrespectability becomes a decided source of irritation.

But no doubt many readers—and it would be strange if it were not so—have picked up this little book expecting to find in it a promise of salvation. No doubt many people pass their days feeling helplessly lost, and are neither ashamed of this petition nor irritated by it; instead they grasp it like a nettle with both hands, and from the depths of their hearts they sigh and cry out, "Yes, save us!" If anyone in this wretched condition reads these words, I can assure him that Christ hears and answers this petition, and that here if anywhere we see the truth of the words: "Ask, and it will be given you . . . For every one who asks receives" (Lk. XI.9-10). If the petition of a lost man for salvation rises up to Heaven among a hundred thousand human requests and reaches God, then He will put aside the other 99,999 and attend to this one out of turn. The cry for salvation goes straight to God's heart. To you distressed souls who are sustained by the one ray of hope—that Christ saves—I want to say this: there is one petition in the Lord's Prayer which could be called the special prayer of the despairing, and this is the seventh and last. It was for your sake that Christ added this petition; it was you He had in mind when He fulfilled it. But He fulfilled it by taking the lost condition of the world upon Himself. The seventh petition is answered on the Cross. It brings us straight to the Cross, and here where it is vouchsafed such a hearing is the only place where we can make this petition. Here there is deliverance from evil, "Christ the Redeemer is here", here on the Cross.

It is a common misconception among Christians that when a man has been saved, then he is "well out of it" in the sense that he then has nothing more to do with perdition and the lost. We learn from the Bible that the very opposite is true. If a man was lost and has been saved, then he really begins to be concerned with the lost, for only then are his eyes really opened to all that perdition means. He then sees aspects of perdition of which he formerly had no idea, and therefore used to pass by unheeding. It is the same thing as with illness. Once a man has had heart trouble, then he really begins to notice how many people feel oppressed when the Fhön wind blows. Or if a woman has had to have one of her kidneys removed, she suddenly realises to her astonishment how many people she knows who also have only one kidney. Or if a man was addicted to a vice, let us say drunkenness, and has found salvation at the foot of the Cross, only then is he given the eyes to see this particular kind of perdition: then with the spirit of a

Samaritan he cannot help seeking out other drunkards in order to show them how he himself was helped. Indeed, we can go a step further: a man who has been saved from some specific evil finds that, much to the annoyance of many people, from now on he cannot help seeing the whole world in a wretched condition. Only the man who has been saved knows and understands that in fact everyone who does not know Christ is lost; indeed his eyes and ears are opened to states of perdition over and above what is human, opened to the "groaning of the whole of creation". And when he prays for deliverance, then this prayer becomes an intercession not only for all lost men, but also for the whole of this groaning Creation. Therefore we are praying for everything that has breath and is wretched without Christ when we say, "Deliver us from evil".

It is even true to say that when a man has been saved in Jesus Christ he can then not see any wrong or any need in this world without being driven to this prayer; that above all the sight of any injustice reduces him to the need and promise of this last petition. He can in fact no longer put up with the wretchedness of this world, with war and famine, disease and earthquakes. He can no longer say that all this is fate and therefore unavoidable. He knows now that in all circumstances of wretchedness in this world there is something we can do: we need not be silent, but can cry out, "Save us! Free us from it!" Once a man has tasted the salvation of Christ, then he will not easily rid himself of hunger and thirst for the better world that is to come; he longs eagerly for that world in which crying shall be silenced and pain shall be no more, and where the service of sin shall be ended and the Devil bound, for there even the last enemy will be trodden under the feet of the Lord. When he prays, "Deliver us from evil", it is this future world where death shall be no more that enters into his spiritual field of vision. Incidentally it is interesting to note the strange gradation of the second half of the petitions of the Lord's Prayer: give us our bread for today—forgive us our sins—preserve us from the Devil—and then: set us free from all of these, set us free from the tempter, from sin, and from bread. This is the prayer for the great, complete, and ultimate end of all wretchedness, the prayer for perfection.

And that has brought us face to face with the surprising fact that when we pray this last petition we are concerned with nothing less than the very end, we are praying that the present form of the world may pass away, just as the early Christians in their affliction used to pray for the passing of the world. That is what we are praying for when we call out, "Deliver us from evil".

But once again this is a source of vexation; more so than ever in fact, especially to all the worldly people who find this world not too bad a place, who will be perfectly happy here indefinitely, and who therefore are still far from thinking about the end of the day's work. Indeed they consider it absurd that there could be another and better world than this, and the possibility that this world might pass away makes them sad: they would love to stay on this planet for a thousand years, because they are living on the sunny side. The only thing that troubles them is that they are growing older every day, and will soon not be young and able to enjoy life any more. For them there is no greater vexation than a community that prays that this world may pass away. But to give up one's eternal inheritance for the mess of pottage of the transitory world is another, even sharper aspect of perdition. And this very form of human wretchedness is included when we pray, "Deliver us from evil".

On the other hand—and this is, of course, only the reverse side of one and the same human being—we have the man who is fed up with this earth, perhaps because he finds himself on the shadowed side of life. As a result he feels like saying goodbye to this world and "putting an end" to his life. This sort of man is tired of life, and dreads every new day, and says, "Sleep is good, death is better, but the best thing would be never to have been born at all"; satiated with life, he longs for the day of his death, and curses the day of his birth. And there is also the man who is bored with life, who continually consults his watch and looks to see whether the longed-for evening is coming soon, and who desperately and ardently yearns for the world to pass away, so that he may fade into nothingness. Admittedly the Christian also prays for the world to pass away, but not because he is sick of it, but because he is filled with hope; not because he is tired of life, but because he is hungry for it, hungry for the better life; not because he longs for death and nothingness, but because he knows of the Resurrection and the Life. In fact it is not the evening and the night, it is the shining morning star that inspires the Christian. The night is far gone, the day is at hand. Those early witnesses did not only pray that the world might pass away; they often added: "May Thy grace come, may Thy Kingdom come".

That is the reason why this final petition of the Lord's Prayer leaves us neither discouraged nor helpless, and does not mislead us into neglecting this world, even though it is a vale of tears. Conversely, if there is anything that spurs us on and gives us strength to fulfill our Christian duty here and now; if there is anything that makes us capable of the final surrender, then it is the knowledge that the Kingdom is coming, and that the end is near. In this connexion let me remind you of a strange phenomenon of life in the country, which any farmer will tell you is true. When a farmer is driving his horse home late in the evening, and darkness comes on, the animal becomes visibly tired, and in the end, however reluctantly, the man has to use his whip. But when the lights of the farm come into view in the distance, the horse pricks up its ears and becomes strangely lively, breaks into a gentle trot which gets faster and faster,

even without the use of the whip, until in the end the farmer
even has to pull on the reins.   The animal scents that its
stable is not far away, and knows that the journey is coming
to an end and that it will soon be at home, hence its sudden
transformation.   It is no different in the case of the Christian
who believes in Advent.   Instead of falling asleep he becomes
lively and "pricks up his ears and breaks into a trot", for
he knows that the end is near.   This explains why we have
the strength to surrender when we see the lights in the
distance and know that it is our home, that there is a home
for us at the end of our journey, and that there is a better
world for which we live in faith, and suffer, if need be.
This is the source of strength to work and readiness to fight.
It may explain why there were a considerable number of
Seventh Day Adventists among the Christian martyrs of
very recent years.   When we think about this old world, we
cannot help feeling the "pull of the earth", but the new
world that is to come has its "pull" too.   The words of
Isaiah are fulfilled in the man who has seen the lights of this
new world shining in the distance: "Even youths shall
faint and be weary, and young men shall fall exhausted;
but they who wait for the Lord shall renew their strength,
they shall mount up with wings like eagles, they shall run
and not be weary, they shall walk and not faint" (Is. XL.30f.).

His Kingdom

THE attentive reader will have noticed that the seven petitions of the Lord's Prayer show us one after the other poverty and need and human frailty. We take the Holy Name in vain, therefore we pray, "Hallowed be thy name". The kingdoms of the earth expand by force; nations rise up against nations and kings against kings; there is war and the tumult of war on every side, therefore we pray, "Thy kingdom come". We disregard the Will of God and set our own self-will against it; we act without respect for God and without fear of Him, therefore we pray, "Thy will be done, on earth as it is in heaven". There are poor people among us; but what is worse, there are people who are dying of cold and starvation in God's world of plenty, therefore we pray, "Give us this day our daily bread". But the greatest evil is sin: nations and individuals perish through their unforgiven sin, therefore we pray, "And forgive us our debts, as we also have forgiven our debtors". Injustice is gaining ground hand over fist; love is growing cold; many people are not only losing their reason, but are on the verge of losing their faith and abandoning hope; these are dangerous times, times of temptation, when even God's elect could come to grief over their faith, therefore we pray, "And lead us not into temptation". But we have seen these six petitions of the Lord's Prayer fused into that final one which is in effect a cry for help: "Save us; 'deliver us from evil' ".

And now the Prayer continues: "For thine is the kingdom".

This introduces a new element: petitions have given

71

way to gratitude, and we are beginning to see something of the mystery of the way in which God hears and answers our prayers. The seven-fold knocking has been heard, and the door is beginning to open a little. We know that when Stephen, the first Christian martyr, collapsed under the stones thrown by his enemies, he saw the Heavens opened, and that in his pain and torment a spirit of praise and thanks came upon him, so that here on earth he was able to do what is usually the function of the angels and the saints in Heaven: Stephen was able to make a prayer of intercession. Something of the kind takes place when a man earnestly prays the Lord's Prayer, when all a child of man can do is kneel on the ground, wring his hands, and knock. Then it can happen that God's first answer to an urgent prayer like this is to send a spirit of worship. And where this spirit of worship comes down, the need is partially overcome already. Worship implies that a prayer has been heard, implies victory, victory in Heaven; and so worship also implies resistance to the principalities and powers. The power of faith can hardly appear more effective than in a man who has been granted the gift of worship. The Name of God may be taken in vain; our self-will may be strong; the powers of this world may be terrible; sin may be powerful; people may be starving; the Devil may be abroad—but nevertheless: "Thine is the kingdom". The "nevertheless" of faith is worship when it appears before the throne of God almighty. Indeed, when Stephen saw the Heavens opened, he saw Jesus standing at the right hand of God, and it is to Christ that we refer when we say, "Thine is the kingdom": to Him the Father has given all things in Heaven and on earth; He lives and reigns; it is He and no other that we mean when we too say in worship, "Yes, Lord; thine is the Kingdom".

It is an historical fact that this glorification at the end of the Lord's Prayer was at first not in general use in the Christian world. The words of praise became established only in the course of the first centuries A.D., at first in individual communities and later everywhere. Certainly this ending is made up of biblical phrases, originating from the Books of the Chronicles, but it was not usually customary to follow up the seven petitions of the Lord's Prayer with these words of praise. Later on, the person who was conducting the service would make the seven petitions to God, and then the congregation would join in with the words, "For thine is the kingdom. . . ."

It is significant and important that it took persecution to establish this glorification in the Christian Church generally. The more martyrs there were, the more wide-spread did these words of praise become. And that gives us an insight into the essence of all worship. Worship is most usually found where men are down and out, where there is suffering, or even dying. At sick-beds and death-beds; in circumstances of economic hardship; among those who are weary and oppressed the spirit of worship is most easily to be found. Strange, but true! It is those who labour and are heavy laden who know best what it means to face the day with nothing, absolutely nothing but praise and gratitude. There are very few things that they want except only to see Him whom Stephen saw in the Heavens and worshipped when he was being stoned: the Lord of the Kingdom. At every time of persecution in the Christian Church worship was a protestation of faith. Glorification is the most lasting and effective protestation of faith against the powers of unbelief. And the words of praise at the end of the Lord's Prayer came to be understood more and more in this sense: the Kingdom is not Rome's, nor Nero's, nor Decius', nor Diocletian's or whatever any of the persecutors of the Church to the present day may have been called: no, not theirs but "Thine is the Kingdom", Thine alone. And the man who more than once looked martyrdom in the face understood it very well too when he said, "Let them take my body, my property, my honour, children and wife;

F

let them all go, they have gained nothing: the Kingdom remains ours—'for thine is the kingdom' ".

That is faith in the Kingdom of God. Let us find out a little about the nature of this faith, for we of today need to do this. First of all we can say that there is inherent in it a deep feeling for the whole. Christ is not only the Lord of spirit and our spirits; He is also the Lord of matter and our bodies. Christ is not only the Lord of the inner world; He is also the ruler of the outer world. He is not only the Lord of the Church, but at the same time the Saviour of the world. He is not content to be Lord of the human world; He also claims dominion over the animal world, over all dumb creatures. In fact Christ is ultimately Lord of the world of angels and the world of the Devil too. So when we worship and glorify Him, saying, "Thine is the kingdom", then we are looking up to Him who is Lord of all creatures in Heaven and upon earth; then we are including Heaven and earth and Hell when we worship before the throne of God. Thus faith in the Kingdom is always a matter of the whole.

Over and against this we have to say that our customary Christian faith has to a great extent become emaciated and consumptive. It has largely shrivelled up into a personal and private matter between God and the soul. Perhaps our faith is deep and fervent, but where does the Kingdom enter into it? We have forgotten that while Christ certainly paid the ransom to save our souls, this same ransom also represents the entrance money into the Kingdom, and the price of eternal citizenship. That is why we must re-learn not only to be children of God and members of His household, but at the same time citizens of God and members of His Kingdom, invested with the privileges and also the duties of eternal citizenship. Only when we have learned that anew will worship take its place again in the Church, for worship and faith in the Kingdom belong together.

A fundamental aspect of the nature of the citizenship of

Heaven is that it can neither be earned nor bought: it can only be given to us as a gift, quite free and undeserved. Faith in the Kingdom goes hand in hand with the words, "By grace alone". We can never become citizens of the Kingdom of God without owing it to Christ. No one can get round this debt. And everyone to whom Christ gives citizenship owes Him gratitude for a lifetime, indeed for eternity. The man who is given this gift by grace can take his part in the Kingdom. This is the great favour bestowed upon those who have become not only children, but at the same time citizens of God. They can join in the work on God's building site. They can take part in the building of His Kingdom, and where the battle for His Kingdom flares up God's fellow workers can fight the good fight of faith. And the most brilliant stars of the promises of the Bible shine on the fellow citizens of God. Under no circumstances will they ever be confounded; they will be harmed by neither humiliation nor honour in this world; they will be saved through fire and water; a thousand may fall at their side, and ten thousand at their right hand, but they will not be harmed; nothing, neither death nor life will be able to separate them from the love of God; their personal needs will be satisfied without thought or effort on their part, as long as their first concern is for God's Kingdom and His righteousness. So they will be delivered from a multitude of cares, and freed from human anxiety and the fear of death; they will enjoy the glorious freedom of the children of God. This priceless, holy freedom is offered here not only to a few, but to us who have let Christ redeem us and pay the price of our place in the eternal Kingdom. What a wonderful thing it is to be able to join in the worship and say, "For thine is the kingdom".

Who would not like to join in? Who would want to go on nourishing a stunted faith that is only personal and fights shy of participation, and that fears unselfish objectivity? Who would want to go on saying that phrase which one hears so often, especially in educated circles: "Of course I'm religious, but the Church doesn't mean a thing to me"? If you are religious, then you join in in one place and you no longer stand to one side as an aloof onlooker: instead you take your responsible share where the cause of Christ is confessed, and in spite of everything that is still the Church for the time being. And now who can still say, "I am religious, but I am not worldly"? If you are religious, and truly religious, then you are also worldly, and truly worldly, and you take a responsible share in the struggle for fair wages and decent living conditions. In fact, if no one were to fight for right and justice but the Communists, then you would let yourself be classed with them, and would join in with them, for "If these were silent, the very stones would cry out" (Lk. XIX.40). Belief in the Kingdom of God means participating, not shirking one's responsibility when right and truth are at stake. Certainly the Kingdom is within you and in the Church too, but it is greater than either. Faith in the Kingdom is comprehensive.

Also related to the nature of faith in the Kingdom is the fact that the greater part of the Kingdom is invisible, and what can be seen is far from splendid. When the Kingdom of God is in battle, then the larger part of the army, its main force, is invisible. In the eyes of this world the Christians are a "little band", but there is a force standing behind those who are here fighting the battle of faith, and that is the unseen warriors of God. This partial invisibility of the Kingdom should neither vex nor trouble us, and above all we must not let it discourage us. The Kingdom in fact exists in this world only in the form of signs. The Church is such a visible sign of the invisible.

In addition to this the Kingdom of God is concerned with the future. Its emphasis is on what is to come and not on what is past. We must take good note of this, we Christians who, unfortunately not without reason, are often portrayed by wicked tongues as back-pedallers, constantly looking backwards instead of to the future. The man who has faith in the Kingdom is concerned with the future: practically speaking, that means that he always arrives a little ahead of time; he always gets up a little too early; and he is living a little before his time. That is why people who have faith in the Kingdom are like flowers which bloom in the early spring: suffering and frost await them. But you who have come a little too soon must not let that trouble you. It is better to arrive a little too early than, as unfortunately used to be the rule with Christians, always a little too late, always a little behindhand, when others have already dared and suffered. Be comforted, you who are a little too early: "It is your Father's good pleasure to give you the kingdom" (Lk. xii.32). Perhaps the world will not understand what you meant until two years afterwards, or perhaps even ten, or twenty, or even a hundred years, long after your life in the visible world has ended: be comforted, you who are too early, the future belongs to you, for the Kingdom is concerned with the future; it is coming.

And the form of the Kingdom must not trouble us either. The Kingdom reflects something of the form of its Lord. We read of Him: "He had no form or comeliness that we should look at him, and no beauty that we should desire him" (Is. liii.2), and we might speak of His Kingdom in the same vein. The Kingdom of Christ is rarely endowed with beauty in this world; it is more often disguised and made unrecognisable by all kinds of ugliness. In the eyes of this world the children of the Kingdom have all sorts of defects in their beauty. But we must not be alarmed because what is wisdom in the eyes of the world is folly in the Kingdom of Christ; because here honour often becomes humiliation and disrepute; because it is a Kingdom of poverty, whose wealth consists of the poor, the sick, the dying, the crippled, and the oppressed. To take part in the building of this Kingdom is to confess in worship: "For thine is the Kingdom".

And one thing more. A few years ago another false message about a false kingdom became widespread. The word "Reich" began to grip the imagination of millions of people. Hundreds of thousands of mothers sacrificed their sons and daughters for this "Reich"; hundreds of thousands gave up all that they had for it. Those who were scattered abroad seemed to have only one longing: to get "home to the Reich". They believed with near-religious fervour in the "Reich" for which they died. And this terrible thing was bound to happen to a generation that had lost sight of the message of the true Kingdom, a generation that knew only its own Godless or zealous soul. An almost demonic hunger to "participate", to stand and fall for a cause, to join in the building of a kingdom, got a frenzied hold on people. But was not the reason for this fearful going astray primarily the fact that the true message of the true Kingdom had been largely withheld from this generation? And what will cure us of false and destructive dreams of kingdoms in the future? Certainly not a purely personal piety, however profound and sincere it may be, but faith in the Kingdom of Christ, acknowledgement of the Kingdom of Christ, willingness to suffer and die in the service of the Kingdom of Christ. Children of God, it is time to become citizens of God.

His Power

terrify

A WORD that can vex or comfort us more than
most other words in the Bible is the word power,
the power of God. Admittedly we do not notice at
the first casual mention of the word that it is capable of
giving vexation: on the contrary, when there is talk of
power modern man pricks up his ears. Power is our
watchword, so to speak, and a subject in which we think
we are particularly well versed. Naturally power is our
primary necessity under all circumstances! Power has
become our dream. In fact we have long since ceased to be
content with human power; we have passed that stage; we
do not want to have the strength of a man, but the strength
of a horse. We have even invented an abbreviation for it:
h.p. In school and workshop our young men become
familiar with horse-power; they learn to think in terms of
horse-power, and to work and travel with horse-power.
In stories of ancient times we read of creatures called giants,
who had special powers; from the Middle Ages we hear of
people who tried their utmost to acquire such super-powers
and to use them for the good or ill of their fellow men.
Those were isolated cases, but today it is everyone who is
striving after the strength of a horse; everybody would like
to be a giant. Power, strength, "strength through joy",
has become the dream of our whole generation, and power
is its idol. Conversely, the man who lacks power is
unfortunate indeed: in an age which idolises power he has
forfeited his right to existence. No wonder that today we
are more afraid of lack or loss of power than of anything
else. This preoccupation with power has penetrated deep

into our Christian faith like a yeast. Even faith is beginning to interest us only in so far as it provides us with the power or strength that we desire and worship, and if our faith denies us this power that is to enable us to compete in this world, then it can be stolen from us. So to the modern man faith has to a great extent become a means to an end, a kind of power-brew, or power-fodder. Unless I am very much mistaken, many of us go to church time and again thinking only of power, strength for the coming week, strength to perform our pressing duties. Certainly strength is not unimportant, and our duties are not negligible, and today the drain on our strength is enormous; but have we not noticed that we have identified ourselves with this century's pursuit of power to the extent that we value faith only as a source of strength, and that in doing so we too have bent the knee to the Baal of the century, the idol of performance, strength, power! But the axe is laid to the roots of this idol when Christ teaches His own to say, "For thine is the power", no one has it but Thou; it is Thine alone.

But now the idolatrous yeast that is so deep-seated in our souls begins to rise once again. It is a fact that even in our prayers and even in the worship that Christ has taught us we cannot help thinking first and foremost of creative power, the powers of nature, the powers in the air, in the water, and in the earth; indeed the spiritual corruption of our day goes so deep that even in church we are constantly tempted, and catch ourselves thinking first and foremost of the powers of creation. In other words, we too are on the look-out for a power that will make the strong even stronger, and the weak a little less weak; in our eyes too this power serves only to strengthen us men. And yet, quite understandably, we are always afraid of powers of this kind. Even if we have not noticed it till now, we would certainly have to recognise today that there is a sinister aspect to this kind of power. The more creative power a generation can acquire for itself, the more dangerous and at the same time the more endangered does that generation become. Power of this kind always turns into force, but force is evil, evil in itself. Therefore we have good reason to be anxious about the powers that this generation is capable of achieving and amassing in the quiet backrooms and laboratories of science. This fear is well founded, for something is wrong, fundamentally wrong, in this tremendous agglomeration of power that is possible today. But what?

Is it not a fact that we men, who bear, create, and receive these powers are corruptible and corrupt? The human vessel is corrupt, therefore it corrupts in its turn all the creative power that is poured into it. An old wine-grower once told me sadly that a fungus had got into his barrels, so that his wine had been spoiled for two years running. In spite of all kinds of treatment of the barrels he had not got rid of it, and he was beginning to think that the fungus had spread to the whole of his cellar and even that his entire house was infected. Yes, there is a fungus in the barrels: that is the trouble. That is why all new wine that is put into our old barrels is spoiled. Something should be done about it. The Church at its best knew this: when it was praying about power it had in mind powers of quite a different kind; it did not think of creative power, nor of the power that comes from the air, or the earth, or the water, or from laboratories, or from the heads or muscles or hearts of men, because all these barrels are diseased: on the contrary, the Church at its best was concerned with a power that comes from somewhere completely different, from one particular source and only from this source, and that is Christ. It is not a matter of powers of creation, but of redeeming power. Christ came down into our world to cleanse the barrels of fungus; Christ cauterised the corrupted vessels. The finger of the Church points to Christ crucified, who atoned for our sins even unto the depths of Hell and ascended into Heaven: it points to Him and Him alone when we pray, " 'For thine is the power'. Thine is the power that purifies our vessels, Thine is the power that renews us by redemption: if a man is in Thee, then and only then is he created anew, then the old, infected vessel and the whole infected cellar are gone and only in Thee is everything renewed—'For thine is the power' ".

However this is the point at which we really notice the full vexatiousness of these words of praise. This defeated and crucified Christ is the Power, He and He alone. His redeeming power consists in the fact that whereas He was indeed overcome, killed, and buried, then—and again this happened only by that grave—then His redeeming power broke out in the victory of Easter as the only source of power. Thine is the power, all power. The power that redeems and leads beyond sin and death is found only in Christ. The Church at its best never forgets this.

But God wants to give this power to His poor creatures in Christ. No less than this redeeming power that overcomes sin and death is what He wants to give to the weak, and this means the weak in the deepest and truest sense of the word, that is the sinful and the dying. He wants it to be a power of publicans and harlots, a power of the weak and backsliding, a power of death-beds and arenas of death, a power in the town of ruins. And that is the kind of power it is. It wants to give itself completely to the man of faith, so completely that a man like Paul can say, "If we live, we live to the Lord, and if we die, we die to the Lord" (Rom. xiv.8), and, "It is no longer I who live, but Christ who lives in me" (Gal. ii.20). Yes, Paul died with Christ, was crucified with Christ, was buried with Christ, and finally— was raised from the dead with Christ, so that now he can boast of his own weakness. So wholly and completely is "thine the power".

But at the same time this is where we really notice the full splendour of these words of praise. Not only is the idol of "power" cast down, but a kind of power is offered here which is "made perfect in weakness" (ii Cor. xii.9).

When a man refuses to be vexed any longer and worships this power in faith, then he is endowed in all his weakness with a power that is so splendid that it could only have come from Christ. We can have reached the stage where we are so tired that we are not refreshed even after a good night's sleep, yet nevertheless, even if we have had a bad night and are utterly exhausted, we can look at the risen Christ and know that the world will not pass away even though we are tired and remain tired, for our spirit cries out in worship, "For thine is the power". So it is no great disaster if we are tired: the disaster would be if Christ were tired, but then He is never tired nor weary, for "Thine is the power". Now we can become quite useless; we can become mental or physical invalids; our duties can pile up like mountains and threaten to crush us. We can have too much to do and too many duties to perform, so that we really are not equal to them any more. And we can suddenly be too old. But through the crucified and risen Christ the miracle of worship can come to us in our weakness, so that even in our frailty we can say, "For thine is the kingdom". We may be like the school teacher who had to retire early because of tuberculosis just when he was about to start with a new class. No doubt he was overshadowed by the dark wing of despair, but someone else had touched him already, and from the broken figure on the Cross the words came to him: "Thine is the power". Even though we may retire from the building site of a new age, the building will go on, for Christ is the Master Builder and His power is unbroken. And further, it can happen that a member of a community who has become blind and lame says, "I cannot even pray properly any more, for the frailty of my old age even affects my prayers"; but "his is the power"; the community is built up nevertheless. For after all this is the building material with which Christ sets up His Kingdom: the blind, the lame, and the sick, sinners and publicans, weak, backsliding people who have to confess,

"We are powerless . . . We do not know what to do, but our eyes are upon thee" (II Chron. xx.12).

But what about the strong? Are they not allowed to participate in the building of the Kingdom? Only because they are strong and healthy? How can they help it? Yes, they are allowed to take part too, but—and now you can be vexed once more—not thanks to their strength, nor thanks to their health, but in spite of their strength and their health. I can assure you that you who are handicapped in life are not the handicapped in the Kingdom of God; and we who are favoured in life are not the favoured in the Kingdom of God; our own strength is not a recommendation there, but rather a disadvantage. What a strange "labour exchange" Christ has opened here in this world with His community! Christ engages the strong too, for He "chastises every son whom he receives" (Heb. xii.6), and breaks his strength, which is only a hindrance in the Kingdom of God after all. Remember how Moses was led to breaking-point before God was able to use him! Both the stalwart Peter, and Paul, a giant in body and mind, were dragged down from their horses before there was a job for them in God's vineyard. Their creative power was broken so that in their weakness the power of redemption might be revealed, "For thine is the power" and this "power is made perfect in weakness". If there is any message that is a source either of vexation and judgment or rejoicing to our generation, then it must be the message of the power that is God's. To begin with it is just made up of words, just a message that we have been able to deliver, but "The kingdom of God does not consist in talk but in power" (I Cor. iv.20). The message of Christ will release power; the words will be transformed into power through the Holy Spirit and through Pentecost. At Pentecost the Holy Spirit caused the message of the Cross and the message of the Resurrection to become power for the anxiously waiting handful of disciples. At Pentecost the redeeming

word becaming redeeming power. And now we can pray
for the Holy Spirit to transform the message into power
for us, but once again not our power, but His. When we
look at the destruction in this world, and above all when
we consider the spiritual emptiness of the Church, we may
often be inclined to despair. We are fortunate indeed if
the miracle of worship comes to us in our weakness; and fortunate indeed if instead of being driven
to brooding inactivity we are driven to prayer, however halting, and to the worship of the power that is not
ours.

In the summer of the year 1911, the stream in my native
village in the Jura dried up as the result of a drought. For
us children it had been the scene of countless games, and
while the grown-ups seemed to accept the disappearance
of the stream as a matter of course, it caused a great stir
among us children: it seemed unbelievable that the stream
should have vanished. Where was it? In our simplicity
we decided to go and look for it. We followed the dried-up
bed of the stream up the mountainside until evening came.
Finally we turned back, our mission unaccomplished, sad,
tired, and afraid that we were going to be scolded. We
had not found the stream, but a few days later something
happened in the Heavens: clouds appeared and rain fell in
torrents. Now the village stream came back! While the
grown-ups seemed to accept this with equanimity too, for
us children it was an occasion of rejoicing: our stream was
there again! Many a stream in village or town has dried
up, yet how calmly people accept its disappearance! Why
do we not become like children? Why are we not frightened
because so many streams have run dry, and because so many
of our Church communities are growing bare and empty?
Let us pray now for the one thing that is needful, for morning and evening rain, for the coming of the Holy Spirit,
so that the dried-up streams of blessing and forgiveness
and the river of life that was given at Easter may begin to

flow again! Let us pray for the one thing that is needful, that the Holy Spirit may transform into power the message of the Cross and the Resurrection, the message which overcomes the world, and death, and hatred, and the Devil; not our power but His.

His Glory

WE must take care not to let this word mislead us
into being unfaithful to this poor earth. In
Switzerland we have a song which is often sung
by men at the graveside of their friends, and which begins
with the words: "A new day will dawn beyond the stars".
The singers evidently want to say that the light of this day
is there beyond the stars already and that whoever has the
grace not to miss the goal here on earth will have his eyes
opened there, so that he will see this eternal day. Certainly
according to what we learn about the beyond from the
Scriptures there is there a day which will never be followed
by night in all eternity, for "God is light" and "in him is no
darkness at all" (1 Jn. 1.5), and in Him there is no alternation
of darkness and light; "Thou coverest thyself with light as
with a garment" (Ps. CIV.2); He "dwells in unapproachable
light" (1 Tim. VI.16). It is the highest wish of all Christians
to enter into this eternal splendour, or, as the original Hebrew
text has it, into this "*kabod*" or "*shekina*". This glory is the
radiance of the eternal majesty of God. There is no source
or spring of glory other than God. Glory is strictly and
exclusively His. "Thine is the glory, for ever and ever.
Amen". This glory is in fact essentially "beyond the
stars". The sun that we love so much and whose light
our eyes cannot even bear, and all those stars which, we are
told, have a much stronger light than the sun; all the
heavenly bodies of day and night are miserable glimmers in
comparison with the brilliance of the eternal glory of our
Father in Heaven. In fact, all created light is not to be
compared with that "uncreated light" that is meant when

the community of Christ says in worship, "For thine is the glory, for ever and ever".

"A new day will dawn beyond the stars." There is something in this belief: let us not despise it, for there is something great in being able to believe that there at least there will one day be light. In these dark days and nights not a few people have found some support in this kind of faith, even if not a very strong support. On dark winter days, when the gloomy blanket of fog hangs so heavy over our homes, we often feel a little brighter if we can tell ourselves that above the blanket of fog the sun is shining in a blue sky. God knows the hearts of the brothers who have derived comfort from faith in the "beloved Father who lives above the canopy of the stars", and who have found support in the words of the prophet: "Arise, shine; for your light has come, and the glory of the Lord has risen upon you. For behold, darkness shall cover the earth, and thick darkness the peoples; but the Lord will arise upon you, and his glory will be seen upon you" (Is. LX.1-2).

And yet we do not always feel quite happy about this belief in the God above us, as He is portrayed in these well-known and well-loved songs. If faith goes no further than this, it can under certain circumstances become something cheap. The song about the God above the stars escapes our lips all too readily and easily, and it is perhaps no accident that such confessions of faith are generally of a somewhat poetic and artistic nature. Songs of this kind sound all very well in the exalted mood of Sundays and religious celebrations, but in our workaday lives they are rather out of touch with reality. Songs about God-above-the-stars tend to fight shy of the many different things that happen under the stars. Does not this ceremonious kind of belief in God often put us ominously in mind of the sort of ruler whose subjects, while honouring and revering him, prefer to have nothing to do with him, and who is

surrounded with solemn pomp, but is kept out of touch with
the real lives of his subjects? Whatever goes on in his
kingdom, the attitude of his people is: "The heavens are
wide, and the Czar is far away". It is not without anxiety
that we ask whether this much-sung God above the stars
might not be one of these rulers estranged from reality.

In fact this belief might well cause us great distress. If
I am down below, really down below, under the stars;
supposing I am lying on the ground at night with broken
limbs, then the cold and distant glittering of the stars could
drive me to despair. What is the use of a distant light
that is even farther away than the stars? Would an injured
man lying down below in the coldness of the night not
prick up his ears if he heard footsteps and saw a light
approaching him, and if a face bent over him—and even if
the tiniest little light were to brighten the place where he
was lying! Even if it were a hundred thousand times fainter
than all the distant starlight and the even more distant light
of God, a light as near as this would be a hundred thousand
times more precious to us, because it would be with us.
And that is exactly what has happened. God was not
content that "A new day will dawn beyond the stars".
God wants to be known for more than merely living above
the canopy of the stars: He wants to come down to us men.
What no star and no sun was able to do, what no poet ever
dreamed of happened and became fact: God came down
from beyond the canopy of the stars. In Jesus Christ the
glory of God is now no longer only above us, but with us.

But when the eternal God came down to us from His
Glory, He was not like people of high rank who, when they
step down from their cultivated milieu, are terribly afraid of
getting their polished shoes dirty and of spoiling their
dainty hands, hardly daring to walk a step or to touch
anything. God did not spare His glory and was not ashamed
to become our earthly brother in every way. He actually
stepped out of His glory. He left Heaven behind; He

G

"emptied himself, taking the form of a servant, being born in the likeness of men" (Phil. II.7). He was not ashamed of us, but came right in among us. He forsook His glory and assumed the direct opposite of what is meant by *"kabod"* and *"shekina"*; and the direct opposite of divine glory is human sin, in other words the darkness that covers both us and the world as a whole. From now on there were supremely happy people who could say and testify in faith, indeed only in faith, "We beheld his glory, glory as of the only Son from the Father . . . full of grace and truth" (Jn. I.14). Christ came into the world, and then day began to dawn under the stars.

When day breaks in this world of creation, the peaks of the mountains are touched with gold first of all. The first rays of the sun fall on the heights. Who has not been awed into silence by the majesty of a sunrise in the mountains! But in the realm of salvation the "sunrise" happens differently. When the glory of God came down to earth it was not the peaks of society in Jerusalem that were the first to be touched with gold: on the contrary, we read of this "sunrise": "There were shepherds out in the field, keeping watch over their flock by night. And an angel of the Lord appeared to them, and the glory (the splendour, the *kabod*, the *shekina*) of the Lord shone around them, and they were filled with fear" (Lk. II.8-9). The glory of redemption begins to shine low down. First of all it touched the shepherds, and from there it worked its way down, deeper and deeper. "When he saw the crowds, he had compassion for them, because they were harassed and helpless, like sheep without a shepherd" (Mt. IX.36). And to the lowest He called, "Come to me, all who labour and are heavy-laden, and I will give you rest (Mt. XI.28), come into the light that is shining for you". He penetrated right down into the pits of human wretchedness, and even the dens of vice were not unknown or barred to Him. He went down into the prisons where neither moon nor stars could shine; He went into the alleys and the cellars; indeed He Himself experienced the darkness of a human grave; and finally the glory of Christ "descended into hell". Not a fraction, not a hair's breadth of darkness did He leave to death or the Devil: day began to dawn as far below the stars as this. Today, when a wave of cold is moving through the nations and a spiritual Ice Age is threatening to set in on earth, today let us hear this message: in Jesus Christ God has come down with the full warmth of Heaven, and Christ is here with the whole shining glory of God, hidden to the eyes, but visible to the spirit. Now, when the cold is in league with the darkness, and a night when no one can work threatens to come, we should not sing about the "beloved Father who dwells above the canopy of the stars": no, now is the time for us to testify in defiance of all outer appearances: "The night is far gone, the day is at hand" (Rom. XIII.12). The glory of God is with us in Jesus Christ.

But, we may well ask, what if all this still means nothing to me? What if I hear the message, yet inwardly remain damp and cold and dark and dead? What if I have to sit here empty today? These questions are justifiable and understandable; in fact it is a good thing that they should be asked. Definite cold or warmth is better than a vague uneasiness, or lukewarm half-heartedness. The Bible provides for the condition of utter cold and darkness. It says that the light shines in the darkness, but that the darkness does not comprehend it. Yes, the Bible anticipates that we men shall have great difficulty with the message of God's glory under the stars, for it assumes that we can grasp this glory only in faith, because it appears on earth in a veiled form. The glory of God is offered to us in a few words, on a sparsely laid table, in poor symbols measured by the standards of this world. And we are lost without faith. But the man who feels that he cannot believe it, and who is therefore troubled and unhappy, can be comforted by the knowledge that in reality faith has already taken root

in him, and that a door has opened and let a chink of light
shine in upon his darkness.

It was not for nothing that before His departure Christ
found it necessary to promise His disciples the Holy Spirit
who "will guide you into all the truth" (Jn. xvi.13). The
man who cannot believe (and who is there who can believe?)
can and should pray for the Holy Spirit. If a man knocks
here, the door will be opened to him and he will not remain
inwardly cold and empty and dead and dark. The glory of
God is now no longer above us, nor only with us; through
the Holy Spirit who brings about faith the eternal splendour
of God miraculously becomes a glory in us whereby the
hearts of men are illumined and become warm and bright.
Quite simply and concretely, this glory of God in us is seen
when a poor sinner is allowed to come to the Table to receive
the symbols of forgiveness; and when a man dies believing
that he will share in eternal life, then the glory of God is
seen in him. Once again we cannot put it more simply and
better than in the parable of the son who was lost and was
welcomed back by his father, that parable that we were
reminded of at every moment and at every turn in the
course of our study of the Lord's Prayer. There where the
father runs to meet his son, where the son's rags are taken
from him and he is given a new robe, and shoes are put on
his feet and a ring on his hand; there where he hears the
words: "This my son was dead, and is alive again" (Lk.
xv.24); there where he is offered a place in his father's
household and at his table, the place he had squandered and
gambled away (all of which happened for the sake of
Jesus Christ, who tells this great story); there the glory of
God the Father shines forth. And it shines forth where the
criminal on Christ's right hand falls silent because at the
hour of death he has heard the words: "Today you will be
with me in Paradise" (Lk. xxiii.43).

When a man has been given the gift of grace by the
Holy Spirit he can see this eternal glory of the Father's

mercy in this world shine forth in and around men, and much more often than you would think. A few weeks ago a girl who had stubbornly defied her aunt for a whole year wrote her a letter of four or five lines to say that she was sorry: the glory of the Father shone forth from this pathetic human scribble. And the majesty of divine mercy lights up that hospital bed where an old man is lying groaning in pain, but at the threshold of death faith shines through his groaning. At an international conference a few months ago the representative of a leading nation withdrew a fully justified claim to the advantage of another country, in order to save the situation which had become quite impossible. There the light of Good Friday and Easter shone into the lives of the nations for a moment. And down below the Minster here in Basle, on the other side of the Rhine, you can see the scaffolding on a war-damaged church tower growing day by day. Six of the men who are rebuilding the tower are German prisoners-of-war, the seventh is a man who has spent some time in a concentration camp: there you can see the glory of God again. The man who is given the gift of faith will realise over and above this that such signs are small guiding lights pointing to the day when the new Jerusalem will come down out of Heaven like a bride adorned for her husband, when there will be no more death, nor mourning, nor crying, nor pain: the street of this city is transparent as glass, and we read that "The glory of God is its light" (Rev. XXI.23). There is no need for moon or sun or star to shine upon it, the eternal splendour is light enough. Here the new day has dawned: here the redeemed, clothed in white robes, together with all the angels and the saints, praise, worship and cry out, "For thine is the kingdom, and the power, and the glory, forever. Amen".

Amen

IT is difficult to ascertain how long the phrase "iron curtain" has figured in the press. Does it surprise us that today every nation barricades itself in its own way behind such "iron curtains" of distrust? Is it not true that this distrust is in fact present in every nation? Is there not a curtain of this kind between our country and the others, which were led along such a terribly different path in the last ten years, and which suffered such a completely different fate from ours? And finally is there not something like a curtain of distrust hanging across the middle of individual nations too? Is it sheer fabrication when there is talk of serious lack of trust between people and government in every country from time to time? Indeed in talking to people of all classes today one feels that each person has his own little iron curtain, so that one cannot avoid having the impression that a certain mistrust is automatically characteristic of modern man. At any rate we cannot be too plainly aware of how precarious the trust between men has become in the past decades. And we often do not realise fully enough what dimensions the spiritual destruction of men has assumed as a result of this disintegration of trust. Is this condition surprising? Surely we do not think that the world can break promises and practise deceit and lies, and then be filled with trust again overnight! We shall not so easily get rid of the spirits of distrust that we were so bent on calling up. We can conjure up the electric light by manipulating a switch, and make it disappear again at our pleasure, but more than that is necessary to switch from distrust to trust. So we must be patient with the great and their great iron curtains, and the small and their small iron curtains. And if nations seem reluctant to trust one another

today, then we must remember that this is one of the
after-effects of a most terrible war. But under no circumstances are we entitled now to gossip about "signs of
another war". Unfortunately it has almost become
fashionable again to talk about "the next war", and there
is nothing cheaper than to join in these ominous rumours.
Going by the present condition of the world, there is nothing
clever in prophesying that there will soon be another war.
Not that we should feel constrained to prophesy the
opposite, but I am of the opinion that everyone who
thoughtlessly plays this tune should be given a philanthropic
box on the ear, for the "next war" will be nothing less
than a disaster. Not in blind confidence, but inspired by
the "nevertheless" of faith let us rather talk of how the great
and small iron curtains could be drawn aside, in spite of all
appearances to the contrary, and of how the distrust that is
so dangerously prevalent on all sides could be overcome, and
above all of how new trust could be implanted in the
pitifully crippled souls of the nations. This replanting may
be difficult enough, like the replanting of a forest after it
has been completely cleared. But have we not seen from
the railway line nearby in Alsace, between Colmar and
Strasbourg, how farmers have recently planted young
trees? And in the ruins of a country village there you could
see a thirty-foot-high gable wall, all that remained standing
of a war-damaged house. Curiously enough, on top of the
wall there was a nest which, according to the local minister,
had been occupied only the day before by a homing pair of
storks. On their return the storks had not found their
house, so they simply settled down on the one remaining
wall, and there they stood now, on one leg, as storks have
done for thousands of years, clattering their beaks and
probably thinking of laying eggs and rearing young in the
near future. Do not throw trust away! Now of all times
do not let distrust get the upper hand! It may be difficult
enough to build new walls and to replant no-man's-land:

how much more difficult to replant areas of devastated trust! But that should not prevent our trying it all the same, even if it has to be done on top of ruins; even the stork lays its eggs and rears its young on top of the ruins! "Look at the birds of the air . . ." (Mt. VI.26).

But if we set about the problem of restoring broken trust, then at first the damage appears worse than we thought, and the difficulties seem to tower up insuperably, so that we are in danger of losing courage completely. What is the fundamental reason why one man does not trust another farther than he can see him? Does not the distrust between man and man ultimately spring from a distrust between man and God? One might envy that stork on the ruin who can only trust in his Creator. Modern man's deepest need is probably that he does not trust in his Creator. Is not trust in the credibility of man's word broken because trust in God's Word was shattered long ago? Has not the atmosphere of mutual trust between men been destroyed because long ago the atmosphere of trust towards God was undermined? Behind all our small and great iron curtains is there not ultimately that one curtain which men have drawn in the face of God since the day when the first man found it necessary and advisable to hide himself from God? Human trust has disappeared because trust in God has disappeared. Our distrust of men stems from that all-destroying scepticism, the cancer of this generation, which in turn stems from the fact that we are no longer children of our Father in Heaven.

Therefore it is trust in God that must be planted again first and foremost. But can we do this? Is it in fact conceivable that we can ever again get to the stage where, shall we say, a group of modern men listen to a sermon no longer as only the opinion of a man that puts them under no obligation, but as the proclamation of the divine Word that is to be taken seriously? Or how can this generation ever be induced to regard the Church not as a kind of consulting room, but as the dwelling-place of the glory of God? And above all, how shall we ever again be in a position (which of us does not long for it with all his heart!) to pray the Lord's Prayer like children and to believe that our prayer will be heard, and thus to believe in the meaning and value of prayer? A generation that is so corrupted by scepticism and distrust towards God that it is incapable of childlike prayer is ripe for destruction. But we do not want to perish; we should like to be able to trust again as strongly and as implicitly as the stork that chose a ruin for its nest; we should like to trust in God and thus conceive new trust in men as well.

Perhaps it will be some help to the reader who is particularly weighed down by this lack of trust in God and who is haunted by the negative spirit of doubt, if we can demonstrate that after all this spiritual attitude is not only a characteristic of modern man. Even if this "spirit that always denies" (Faust) has spread its poison more widely than ever today, this disease of the soul should not be looked upon as a phenomenon of the twentieth century. It has always existed; it is known and mentioned in the Bible, where we see the appearance of this disease almost as early as man himself. We read about Sarah laughing to herself when one of the greatest promises of the Old Testament was made, namely that in her old age she would bear a son who would be the ancestor of countless descendants. The Bible also shows us a people in the wilderness who murmured and wept instead of giving praise and thanks when they were given information about the Promised Land by the men who had spied it out. And on the very threshold of the New Testament, when the angel announced that a new age was about to begin, Zechariah shook his hoary priest's head in doubt. And at Easter, when the miracle of all miracles happened, Thomas vowed that he would never believe the fabulous news of the Resurrection of Christ. So we meet the disease of doubt at every turn in the Bible itself, and so God knows our distrust towards Him and takes human doubt seriously. But even though man's unbelief is called sin throughout the Bible, God does not meet it with uncomprehending severity, but in love and with Fatherly patience. God sees that our sin is at the same time our need; He takes it into account and He intends to help us.

One indication that God has pity on our lack of faith is, among other things, the existence of that so well-known yet so mysterious word: "Amen". And now I am going to make an assertion which may sound bold and arbitrary; but the longer we consider it, the more clearly shall we recognise its truth. If this generation could once again not only say the Lord's Prayer like a child, but could also say "Amen" in prayer, then it would have won trust in God. It would mean that a small shoot of trust had taken root again; that the first little flower of trust in God was planted, the first furrow ploughed, and the first seed-corn full of hope set in the arid soil of the earth. It is of the utmost importance now for this generation to learn that it could be given the gift of being able to say "Amen" once more.

But what is so significant about this word? In the Gospels we meet it only on the lips of Jesus: we hear it spoken by no one but Him. More than two dozen times He introduces His words with this striking *"Amen, Amen, lego hymin"*, a phrase with which every reader of the Bible is familiar: "Truly, truly, I say to you". Thus this "Amen, Amen" is an assurance that He is speaking not for Himself but by order and with authority as the ambassador of the Father. The Old Testament phrase that approximates to it in meaning is that confirming and at the same time adjuring introduction generally used by the prophets: "Thus says the Lord", or "The word of the Lord came to me". And in fact Christ is humbling Himself when he too uses this assurance. As if He needed to emphasise Himself and His

cause with formal recommendations! As if His simple
Word were not sufficient and eminently credible without
His having to say, "Truly, truly, I say to you"! But then
He is saying it for our sake, and for the sake of our unbelief
and our weakness, simply because He is reckoning with
our doubt and lack of faith. Fundamentally therefore it is
not His Word but us wavering men that He is supporting
and reassuring. As surely as God is God and Christ the
envoy of God, so surely do His words come from God.
"Amen, Amen", means truly, truly, it is so, it is valid,
it is true and real. Therefore this "Amen" is in itself a
sign of His mercy which does not disown the man who
doubts, but gives a helping hand to our weak trust in God.

We men too are familiar with ways of adding authority
to what we say: we give our word of honour; or we assist
the credibility of what we write with a signature or a seal,
or we may even go to the extent of taking an oath. Jesus
expressly renounces all these human means of assurance:
He uses neither word of honour nor oath; His own, peculiar
assurance is: "Amen", truly, it is valid. But strictly speaking,
only Jesus is allowed to talk like this: only He who was able
to say, "I am the truth" can say, "Amen, Amen, truly,
truly" in the proper sense of the word. This authoritative
introduction to His words must have been one of the most
annoying and infuriating things about the Man of Nazareth
in the eyes of His enemies. This "Amen" is Jesus' royal
seal that is valid in His Kingdom. Amen, it is so, truly.

All the more surprising therefore is the fact that con-
fronts us at the end of the Prayer which Jesus gave to His
community at the hands of His disciples, for the concluding
word is "Amen". The Lord does something unheard of:
He hands over to His own the seal of His Kingdom, His
Amen, for their own use. Elsewhere He authorises them to
heal the sick, to drive out unclean spirits, and to carry His
name before Kings; and now He gives them the authority
to use His word "Amen". Once again this brings us face

to face with the condescending grace of God. The Amen becomes the express gift of God to us men. A short time ago I met a friend who is in business, and who had just been given the authority to sign documents legally in his employer's name: he and his family were naturally very happy about this: but just imagine what it means when Christ allows men to use His Amen here at the end of the Lord's Prayer! Does this not amount to giving His own a position of trust and authority in His Kingdom? In His mercy He risks giving His Amen into the mouths and hearts of us men. Who does not feel happy and confident when he hears this? And Christ did not hand over His Amen to us on His own account; in this too He let Himself be directed, and only took this step in complete accordance with the Word of His Father in the Old Testament. For there too there were special moments when God allowed and commanded His people to say, "Amen". In fact, every time this happened in the Old Testament it was by the express permission and command of God: "Let all the people say, 'Amen'" (Ps. cvi.48). Since Christ gave the Prayer of His Kingdom to His own, the community of believers in the New Testament are also allowed to say the Amen that only God can give and take away. We feel like a child who has been given an almost terrifyingly precious object to hold; we men who are fickle and lacking in faith are allowed to pray, "Our Father who art in Heaven"— Amen, truly! "Hallowed be thy name"—Amen, truly! "Thy kingdom come"—Amen! "Thy will be done, on earth as it is in heaven"—Amen, truly, it is so, it is valid. In this way Christ implants trust in God in a world sick with scepticism and doubt.

But can the community accept this gift? Is it not too great and precious for human beings? The Apostles dared to do it; they took the gift from the hand of their Lord and boldly handed it on to those who believed. But note how carefully the Apostles themselves pointed out again

and again the association with Christ, and what pains they
took to ensure that this connexion between the Amen and
Christ, between gift and giver should not be overlooked.
They knew that the servant should not regard himself as
the master. In his preoccupation with this we hear Paul
say to the Corinthians, "All the promises of God find their
Yes in him. That is why we utter the Amen through him,
to the glory of God" (II Cor. 1.20). That means that it is
Christ who stands behind every Yes and behind every
Amen, and only in so far as Christ stands behind them are
they not mere empty shells. Indeed, in the last book of the
Bible, where we see all kinds of ruin and destruction and
a world in which distrust has gained the upper hand, we
read something that is surprising in our context: "The
Amen, the faithful and true witness" (Rev. III.14). Who
can this mysterious "Amen" be but Christ Himself! Christ
Himself is the Amen. So if the community says "Amen"
at the end of the Lord's Prayer, then it is speaking nothing
less than the name of Christ, and setting His sign at the end
of the Prayer so to speak. Because of Christ and His
Incarnation; because of His Crucifixion, His Resurrection,
and His return, all God's promises are "Yes and Amen".
Usually it is annoying and humiliating to have to say
"Yes and Amen" to all and sundry: quite rightly we do
not put up with that. But in connexion with the work
and person of Christ we are glad to do it: in this case it is
the gift of all gifts to be able to say "Yes and Amen". "Give
us this day our daily bread"; see how many people on earth
are hungry and lack the necessities of life; do give it to us;
force men's hearts and open their hands, so that soon no
one will have to go hungry any more on this rich earth of
Thine; give us our daily bread—Amen. "And forgive us
our debts, as we also have forgiven our debtors"—Amen,
it is so, we have been forgiven already, for it is fulfilled.
"And lead us not into temptation"—Amen, in Christ the
Tempter is vanquished. "But deliver us from evil"—

Amen: even this comprehensive petition contains its answer in itself: He will deliver us from all evil, for He has the goal of this world in His hand. Christ Himself is the one who is "the Amen, the faithful and true witness".

The regular reader of the Bible must be struck by the joy and enthusiasm with which the communities of the New Testament confirm, accept, and use this gift. When one member of a group of early Christians prayed, the others used to join in with the "Amen". And when one man spoke words of praise, his brothers in faith would answer "Amen" almost before he had finished. And when one of them was inspired to speak, as often as not his words were constantly punctuated by the "Amen" of the community. And so the "Amen" inspired by the Holy Spirit continually bore the words up to Heaven like angels' wings. Thanks to this abundant use of the Amen, the services were rather different from those we know today. The congregations did not sit there silently as if they were not taking part. Any man who was not able to teach or preach could at any time join in with his Amen of faith when the Spirit moved him. Through this confirming Amen inspired by the Spirit, a special kind of communion arose between the speaker and those who were listening, and among the listeners themselves. The communion that came about in this way was similar to what we can see today in quite different, more worldly spheres, such as in the world of sport. The preacher of today is in such a solitary position in his pulpit. Even though he knows that he is accompanied by many a silent Amen, how lonely he is when the community sends him into battle. We should take an example from the children of this world. Have you never noticed what touching concern they show for their champions and how anxious they are about them when they send them on to the field? And have you never seen tens of thousands of supporters shouting encouragement when they watch their team at a football match? But the champions that so many Church communities today send into the arena, into class, into the assembly, into the pulpit, to the sick bed, and to the crematorium are so very much alone. Things were different in the communities of the New Testament. The Christians in Ephesus, Corinth, or Rome were not giving cheap applause; no, each one of them was taking an active part in the battle of the Spirit and the spirits with his contributory and supporting Amen. What a power of rejoicing when a crowd of believers confirm a prayer of thanks with their Amen! And what a power of repentance and atonement when Christians hear words of admonition and judgment, and acknowledge and accept them with an Amen instead of shaking their heads in protest and indignation! And how effective condemnation and blessing are when all those present join in with their intercessional or protective Amen! If only our fellow Christians up and down the land would begin to participate in the Sunday service at least as enthusiastically and wholeheartedly as the spectators at an ice-hockey match! I am sure that this Amen is already spoken softly here and there in the congregation; but what is there to prevent its being said out loud? Do you not believe with me that this Amen which is given by God and inspired by the Spirit could be the "favourable wind" that, amongst us at least, might blow aside many a dividing curtain? Yes, it is the One who is Amen, the faithful and true witness, whom we can trust to have the power to break through the great and small iron curtains. And from the Bible we know that not only the crowd of believers here on earth, but also the multitudes of angels and saints in Heaven join in saying, sighing, and rejoicing: "Amen!" "For thine is the kingdom"—Amen! "And the power"—Amen! "And the glory, forever"— Amen—Amen!